Bungee Jumping

Bungee Jumping
For Fun and Profit

by Nancy Frase

Illustrations by David Gross

ICS BOOKS, Inc.
Merrillville, Indiana

BUNGEE JUMPING FOR FUN AND PROFIT

10 9 8 7 6 5 4 3 2 1

Printed in U.S.A.

PUBLISHER'S NOTE

The sport described in this book is an inherently dangerous activity and any person, especially if inexperienced, undertaking it should approach it with caution and under appropriate supervision. The publisher cannot accept responsibility for any accidents, injury, or loss suffered by any reader of this book however that may be caused.

Published by:
ICS Books, Inc.
One Tower Plaza
107 E. 89th Avenue
Merrillville, IN 46410
800–541–7323

LIBRARY OF CONGRESS CATALOGING-IN-PUBLICATION DATA

Frase, Nancy.
    Bungee jumping for fun & profit / by Nancy Frase ; illustrations
by David Gross.
        p. cm.
    Includes index.
    ISBN 0-934802-81-5 : $12.99
    1. Bungee jumping.   I. Title.   II. Title: Bungee jumping for fun
and profit.
GV770.27.F73   1992
797.5--dc20   92-7104
                                                   CIP

DEDICATION

This book is dedicated to my two lifelong heroes; in memory of my dad and kindred spirit, who passed away unexpectedly during the writing of this book on November 24, 1991; and in honor of my mom, who is the strongest, gentlest, most generous and loving woman I know.

TABLE OF CONTENTS

Preface

Dear Readers,

The purpose of this book is to provide the layman with a comprehensive understanding of the world of bungee jumping. Currently, the only other available information is often piecemeal, biased, conflicting, or highly technical. If you are trying to gain the knowledge of what questions to ask as a potential customer, or if you are considering opening a bungee site, you are likely frustrated by the lack of readily available and understandable data.

The information in this book is presented in a manner that you will find thought provoking, enlightening, and thorough. It is the type of book that you walk through with a highlighter or a pen and note pad. Please take notes. This is a textbook.

The information is organized in a manner that allows you to quickly grasp a general concept and then further study the details as needed. The first chapter defines the sport. The second chapter serves as a shopping guide for a potential site customer. The subsequent chapters are topic specific and intended for focused study. Each chapter ends with a summary to assist you in answering particular questions. An index and glossary are also provided.

The book was written mainly for use in the United States; however, the information is useful to a world-wide audience. It is designed to prepare you to interface with the government agencies, with equipment distributors, and with all the other people associated with the sport. It is not designed to do your homework for you. There is considerable research and engineering beyond reading this book. This book will guide you on engineering issues, concerns to be researched and where to get specific answers as they pertain to your situation.

You are responsible for obtaining professional and qualified instruction before participating in the sport of bungee jumping. This book is only a guide and does not replace that essential instruction. That fact can not be stressed enough. There is not sufficient direction in this book alone to operate a private or commercial bungee site. The contents of this book provide a map for the trip into the world of bungee jumping.

If you have experienced a bungee jump, you understand the impact a single jump has on your life. It has been one of the most powerful confidence builders of my life, and I believe many of you can relate to that. If you are anticipating your first jump, best wishes for a positive experience and welcome to the gang!

After an addicting first jump, my initial involvement in the industry was when I started searching for information to open my own site. I was frustrated by the tight lips of industry members, and the conflicting information. So, I started a newsletter as a way to communicate with other bungeeists. The newsletter's subscriber base grew quickly, and from the newsletter came an association. My focus was to provide the newsletter readers and the association members with the most up-to-date information that I could find. That research prepared me for the writing of this book.

The biggest challenge of this project has been keeping up with the industry developments. This sport has blossomed overnight, and even now it is growing and changing every week. It is exciting to be on the cutting edge. The view is awesome!

Thank you for reading *Bungee Jumping for Fun-n-Profit*. Happy trails as you study the contents and develop an understanding of the world of bungee jumping. May your rebounds be all you wish for!

—Nancy Frase

ACKNOWLEDGMENTS

Special thanks to my personal cheerleading squad who told me to get off my tailend more than once. Thank you to Mary, Toots, Karen, Lil, Peter, The Ogre, Jeff, Jack, and Nogo.

CHAPTER ONE

Introduction to Bungee Jumping

With sweaty hands, Larry Parrish cinched the harness tighter around his hips before climbing into the basket of a hot-air balloon Thursday morning.

His assignment: ride the tethered balloon up 150 feet and jump out, counting on the 50-foot-long rubber bands hooked to the harness to snatch him away from the ground in midplunge.

Enthusiasts of this fast-growing daredevil activity call it bungee jumping. Almost everyone else calls it crazy.

At the count of three, Parrish whooped, stretched out his arms and leapt into the air.

As he plummeted toward a grassy field in far southeast Kansas City, the elastic stretched to 100 feet. Then—boing!—he shot back up. He yoyoed several times, then dangled, as if suspended by a giant umbilical cord.

When his quivering legs were back on solid ground, Parrish, 38, wiped sweat off his face, but nothing could remove his big smile.

"It's always just horrifying" he said, "but that's the *jazz*."[1]

INTRODUCTION

The new sport known as bungee jumping is sweeping the world like wildfire. However, ask the average person walking down the street a question about bungee jumping and chances are his knowledge will include, at most, the basic definition of the sport.

The purpose of this chapter is to provide general information needed to develop a foundation of knowledge about bungee jumping. The following chapters will build on that foundation.

Bungee jumping is the sport of jumping, while attached to elastic cords, from a high platform. The cords allow the jumper to free fall toward the earth and then snatch the jumper back up before he hits the ground. Several falls and rebounds occur before the jump is completed.

Bungeeing is a modern day answer to a certain primal urge. Humans have an inborn desire to experience the intense rush of adrenaline. Bungee jumping provides that rush. There is something magnetic about looking death in the face and laughing. There is something desirable about forcing the body to do what is absolutely against gut-level human nature. There is something stimulating about walking away from a jump feeling bullet-proof. The arousing range of emotions that a jumper feels as he anticipates, then launches into, and finally looks back on his brush with hara-kiri causes a lasting physical high. The various emotions are inevitable, intense, and hit with machine gun speed.

A jumper looks down at the ground and questions his ability to take that plunge over the edge. The platform appears to be at least three times higher than it was when viewed from the ground. The jumper experiences overwhelming terror and decides the whole idea was quite ridiculous. His mother was right. This jumping stuff is pushing fate too far. Who needs to be macho, anyway?

The crowd below begins the dreaded countdown. Count five produces a silent "no way!" Four renders the realization that now is too late to chicken out, three gives birth to bent and shaking knees. On two, the "no way! turns to "oh, well!". Count one causes a numbness, a sort of protective disassociation with reality. Then comes "JUMP!" Somehow, the jumper manages to lean out, but the hands won't let go. After an eternity, the hands receive their delayed instructions from the brain, and turn loose.

Blinding white horror takes the brain hostage and every muscle in the body strains to climb unsuccessfully back onto the platform. When the platform is undeniably out of reach, the jumper is startled to find the ground arriving to meet him at a rather brisk speed. A logical human response to this situation would be a very loud scream. However, the jumper has forgotten to breathe since sometime during the countdown. Count two, to be exact.

The cord begins cradling the jumper to a slower rate, and time begins returning to a more normal speed. Events from this point on are slightly anti-climactic. In trade-off, the emotions are far more pleasant. The jumper realizes that he is not going to hit the ground and that the equipment performed flawlessly. He takes his first breath. And screams. And screams again for good measure.

He stops falling, pauses for half a second, then feels the war going on between gravity and the cords taunt with stored energy. The cords win, and the lazy journey back to the sky is underway. However, lazy is only descriptive of the first few feet, then rocketing becomes the suitable adjective. The jumper's commitment to the upward ride is usually an unwilling one at this point. Especially when gravity finally claims the victory. The jumper reaches a height close to his launching height, and is once again suspended for half a second. He finds himself wishing he could hang on to something during the time of absolute weightlessness. That seems to be a luxury no one remembered to provide.

The downward ride is friendly this time. In fact, the final few bounces are over too quickly. The jumper feels entitled to say anything he wishes at this point because no one is tough enough to stop him as he swings back and forth on the end of the cords. In a few moments, he stands on the ground and greets his fellow jumpers and the cheering crowd with obnoxious whoops. This is what is known as feeling bullet-proof, and it feels GREAT!

To provide a better idea of what happens to a person during a jump, the following is a diagram of the path of the jumper (Figure 1-1)[2]. Notice the initial fall and rebound. They are usually relatively vertical. The subsequent three to five bounces tend to be more horizontal in nature, as well as slower and milder.

Figure 1-1 Path of a jumper during a bungee jump from bottom.

Bungee jumping is often confused with a similar sport known as BASE jumping. The New River Gorge Bridge in West Virginia is the best known location for this sport. Each year on "Bridge Day", a group of people get together to BASE jump. They jump off the bridge wearing skydiving equipment. As they leap, a cable that they are attached to opens their parachute as soon as the jumper is far enough below the bridge to have sufficient clearance. Then the cable swings free of the jumper. He then parachutes the 800 feet to the bottom of the gorge.

One of the most common questions asked by potential jumpers concerns the intensity of the jolts during the jump. To an onlooker standing on the ground, it appears that the jumper experiences a tremendous jolt at the beginning of the initial rebound, and again at the beginning of the second fall. However, the jolt is not as severe as it looks to a spectator. Two reasons account for that. One, the entire body is involved in the movement. The whole body is free to absorb the shock, so no one limb or joint takes the full impact of the jolt. While the body spins quickly, it does so as a single unit.

The second reason is that the person gradually slows to a stop before changing directions. There is not a sudden reduction in speed. The jumper picks up speed during the first half of the initial fall. Then he slows during the second half as the cords stretch. Just before he reaches the bottom of the fall, he is traveling at near zero speed. (Figure 1-2)

The jumper begins his rebound very slowly. Again, he picks up speed until the half-way point. After the half-way point, he slows to hang suspended in mid-air, then starts his second fall.

The total time a person is required to invest in a jump varies greatly. Some commercial jumping sites require training prior to the jump. This training may include a supplemental seminar on related subjects or may be limited to a simple two minute explanation of procedures.

The bare bones training for the jumper at a commercial site is minimal, assuming the site operator is responsible for the equipment and general operations. The jumper's basic single responsibility will be to let go. Gravity and the cords take care of the rest. As the jumper gains more experience, he may wish to add fancy maneuvers to his jumping, which does require more skill.

During the training, a site should include an explanation of what is expected of the customer, and what can be expected of the site operators. Waiver forms may be produced for signatures. Information may be provided on the safety features of the equipment. Most training is done the same day as the jump.

Each commercial jump site has different procedures for placing the equipment on the jumpers. Some sites have the customers don their equipment during the pre-jump training and remain for the entire jumping event. That, of course, requires more time than if jumpers are trained and suited up one-by-one as they arrive at the jump site.

The actual jump is the least time-consuming portion of the experience. The time from when the jumper leaves the ground for the ride up to the jumping height until his feet are back on the ground can be anywhere from two to fifteen minutes. The ride upward usually lasts about one minute, the initial fall about two to eight seconds, subsequent rebounds and falls about thirty seconds, and the return ride to the ground about one minute. Those times allow for a very smooth operation with no reluctant jumpers.

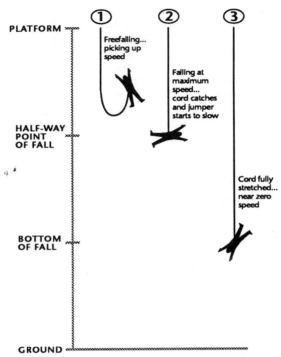

Figure 1-2 Speed of a jumper during the initial fall.

Another common question is about the height of the jumping platform. There really are no limits on a height of a platform. Anything that cords can be attached to and that has the clearance underneath it to allow the movement of the jumper can be used as a platform. It is easy to see how creative thinkers have had a heyday with this flexibility. A fifty foot bridge is a potential platform as much as is a hot air balloon free flying at ten thousand feet. A key point here is that while many objects are potential platforms, they are not necessarily legal or safe platforms. One purpose of this book is to provide guidelines on how to know if a platform is a safe and legal one.

Generally, the height of commercial jumping platforms ranges from fifty feet to three hundred feet. Fifty feet is plenty high for many jumpers. It provides the adrenaline rush without the terror being as overwhelming as with higher platforms. One hundred and fifty feet is a scary enough height for most beginning-jumper adrenaline junkies. Three hundred feet usually will scare even the toughest repeat jumpers.

Some of the most common jumping platforms include hot air balloons, bridges, cranes, and various towers. Bridges were initially the favored platform because they required the least preparation and were plentiful. Also, the bridges provided the clearance needed for the jumper's path of travel.

However, jumps from bridges had to be done covertly since the jumpers could be charged with trespassing. Large fines and a few nights in jail did not produce the adrenaline rush most jumpers desired. It didn't take long for the government and railroad companies to catch on to the covert activities. So, jumpers had to either purchase the bridges or find a new platform.

Tethered hot air balloons caught on next. Since balloons were privately owned, no one could holler about trespassing as long as the land owner obliged. Yet, problems arose with the balloons. Balloons can only be flown during very limited times of day, mainly sunrise and sunset. They are also weather dependent, limited to times of no rain, snow, or wind above a slight breeze.

The Federal Aviation Administration (FAA) had their opinion about using balloons for this sport. Since engineering data was scarce, they attempted to stop the use of balloons for bungee jumping until more information was available. The FAA was concerned that the modifications and extraordinary use might compromise the airworthiness of the aircraft. It was a legitimate concern since the FAA is responsible for insuring the airworthiness of balloons.

During the time the FAA was conducting their investigation of the sport, members of the bungee industry wondered if the FAA would ever approve the use of the balloon. For that reason, and problems from the weather dependency, bungeeist started looking for yet another platform. Construction cranes became a popular choice.

Cranes are not weather dependent and are private property. Alas, this allows for largely unlimited business hours and no trespassing charges. The negatives of jumping from cranes include the incredible start-up capital required, lack of liability and casualty insurance, and the regulations set forth by the Occupational Safety and Health Administration (OSHA). These obstacles are proving to be minor, and cranes are currently the platform of choice from the commercial standpoint.

In short, bridges still remain a common platform. Some bridges are privately owned. Some locations do not forbid the use of public bridges. Some bungee businesses still operate covertly. Tethered hot air balloons can now be used since the FAA has provided a way for bungeeists to obtain the FAA's certification of the balloon's airworthiness. Cranes are quickly becoming the platform of choice. One other type of platform is a tower. The term "tower" is used loosely, and usually it means any stationary platform that doesn't fit in the other three categories. Towers may be made out of any material, be any height, and be designed in any fashion.

HISTORY

Legend has it that bungee jumping first came into being on the Pentecost Island in the New Hebrides of the South Pacific. Prior to World War II, the natives were almost completely isolated. During the war, some of the natives assisted the U.S. Army on Espiritu Island, a sister island. The natives' practice of diving from a tower was introduced to the world through a 1955 *National Geographic* article by Irving and Electa Johnson. Another *National Geographic* article was written in 1970 by Kal Muller on the same group of people.

Muller wrote that according to legend, a domestic dispute was the catalyst for the first jump. An island native, Tamalie, mistreated his wife and she ran away. Trying to hide, she climbed into a high banyan tree. He found her, and climbed up after her. As he was climbing, she tied lianas vines around her ankles.

When he tried to grab her, she jumped out of the tree, and he jumped after her. It seems she was smarter than Tamalie since he had no way to keep from hitting the ground and she did. Tamalie plunged to his death.

The remainder of the men decided that a woman would never get the best of a man again, so the men of the village of Bunlap begin practicing diving with lianas. In the late 1960s, they built an eighty-three-foot tower by binding logs together. Each man was responsible for building his own platform on the tower, and preparing his own lianas.

The day before the big jump, the ground around the tower was softened to create about ten inches of mud. Then, the day of the jump, each man had a ritual bath, climbed to their platform, and tied the vines on their ankles. Then their wife, who had not been allowed in the jumping area prior to this time, was brought to the foot of the tower. She was required to listen while the husband gave his "talk-talk" to vent his complaints against her.

Finally, the men jumped headfirst. The bravest of them jumped from eighty feet, the others jumped from lower platforms. As designed, the vines stopped the men as their foreheads brushed the ground. Alas, the tradition of jumping from high platforms had begun. Its purpose evolved into ensuring a rich harvest of yams. It has since become a tourist attraction for visitors to the islands.

People in other countries took the jumping concept and added a few high-tech features. On April Fools' Day 1979, the Oxford Dangerous Sports Club of Britain, attached themselves to elastic bungee cords and leaped off the 245-foot Clifton Bridge in Bristol, England. This same group jumped off the Golden Gate in California, and then in 1980, bungeed from the Royal Gorge Bridge in Colorado, one of them falling 800 feet with a 415-foot cord and setting a world record.

That world record was broken by John and Peter Kockelman of Mountain View, California. These two were already well-known from their 1990 controversial television commercial for the Reebok shoe company. The commercial showed both of them jumping from the 187-foot bridge at Deception Pass, near Seattle, Washington. John is wearing Reebok Pump shoes and survives the jump in world-class form. Peter is wearing a competing manufacturer's shoes, which are hanging empty at the end of the commercial.

The brothers broke the 1980 record in the spring of 1991. John jumped with a five-hundred-foot bungee cord at five thousand feet from a hot air balloon piloted by Peter.

Commercial bungee sites started appearing around 1986 in various European countries. The first commercial site in the United States began business in 1989, owned by the Kockelman brothers. There are also commercial sites in New Zealand, Australia, France, Germany, Norway, Canada and South Africa.

PLATFORMS

Bridge

The bungee jumping system has relatively few components. They include the platform, cords, harnesses, and carabiners. Carabiners are the metal rings that link the other components together. A platform can be a bridge, hot air balloon, crane or tower. People have also jumped from auditorium ceilings and billboards. Creative minds will surely come up with other platforms.

The bungee platform that is the most readily available is the bridge. However, at this time in the United States, it is illegal to jump from public bridges except in Oregon and Washington states. Many covert jumps have been made from bridges. Those jumps are usually done in the dimness of the early morning with people stationed to watch for the authorities. The location is divulged only at the very last minute.

When a commercial site is operated in an undercover manner, it is the customers who suffer the most. If the group is discovered by authorities, they are subject to steep fines and possibly jail time. Not only that, the customer has no way of checking the safety record of the bungee company's operation. The covert operation of a commercial site may indicate that the owners are not willing to invest the time and money required to provide the safest and most positive experience possible. Site operators who are in the venture for a quick buck, known as "cowboys", can easily use the secretiveness to cover their lack of experience, permits, insurance, compliance to industry guidelines, responsibility for accidents, and inspections by qualified outsiders of procedures and equipment. "Cowboys" give the legitimate operators a bad reputation since the public only knows the locations of the legitimate operations.

Not all bridge bungee jumping is illegal. Most sites in the two states that allow bridge jumping operate legitimate sites. And in states other than Washington and Oregon, some bungee owners own the bridge, or have special permission to jump from the bridge.

A common question about bridges concerns the return of the jumper to the ground. Basically there are two ways to get the jumper off the cord, take him up or take him down. If a jumper is raised back to his jumping point, considerable manpower is required. A motorized pulley system could be used, or a simple system of a few pulley wheels and large number of people pulling on a rope. The benefit of raising a jumper is that if the pulley system fails, the jumper simply falls back onto the bungee cord and gets a free jump. (Figure 1-3)

If a jumper is lowered, the bungee cord has to be disconnected from either the jumper or the bridge. Therefore, the back-up of the bungee system is taken away and the jumper is at the mercy of the pulley system. On the other hand, lowering the jumper cooperates with gravity and requires minimal energy. (Figure 1-4)

If the height of a bridge is great enough that it is extremely difficult to raise the jumper, lowering him is the only option. If the bridge is over water, the jumper could be lowered into a boat. If the water is moving rapidly and it would be dangerous to attempt landing the jumper in the boat, then raising him is the only option.

Jumpers often ask if it is more dangerous to jump from a bridge built over dry land than it is to jump over water. It is true that water gives way to a solid body quicker than firm ground does. However, if the water is only 5 feet deep, the difference seems an insignificant factor if the body is free falling from 250 feet at a maximum velocity of 90 miles an hour. If the body of water is deep, then the water could be a lifesaver. Statistics show that the chances of a bungee system failing at a quality site are slim.

Some commercial sites offer the privilege of being dunked into a body of water as part of a bungee jump. It is difficult to condemn or support the maneuver, or any other similar stunt. The author personally would not do it at a commercial site, but has no right to pass judgment on others who do. Before exercising the option to be dunked, consider the following. Stuntmen who enter the water as part of a show have spent many hours calculating and practicing to figure the exact distance they will fall. They are paid to accept the extra danger. They are aware of all the factors and how they constantly change. At a commercial site, only a few minutes are spent on calculating each customer's jump. A general formula is used that does not allow for changing factors. The fall can differ as much as ten feet from the following changes: air temperature and humidity at 6:00 a.m. vice 10:00 a.m., elasticity of the cord after fifty jumps vice eighty jumps, a slight breeze vice still air, or a feet-first jump vice a swan-dive.

What happens if a site operator misreads the weight scale and provides the jumper with an additional three feet of cord, allowing an extra six feet of drop? What happens if a log happens to be floating in the river where the jumper is supposed to enter? What happens if there is an error of six feet and the water is only four feet deep or if there is a strong current two feet under the surface?

At most sites, the higher a platform is, the more distance is allowed for a margin of error. So if a jumper is dunked from a high bridge, he is being placed in considerably more danger than from a low bridge.

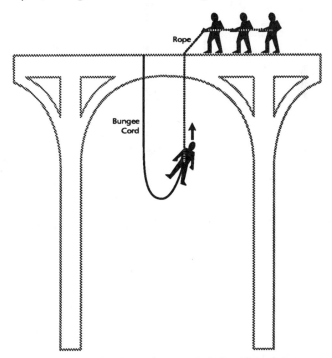

Figure 1-3 A jumper being pulled back up to the jumping platform after a jump.

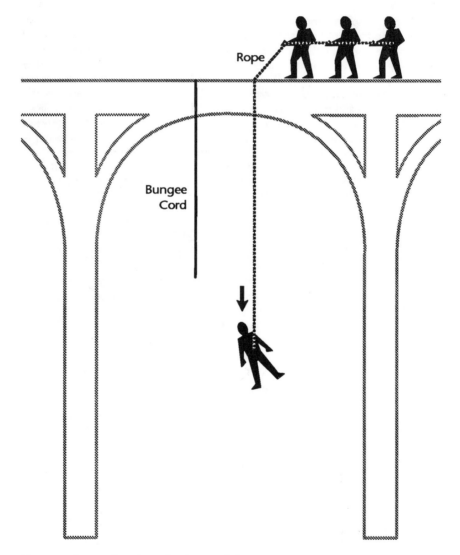

Figure 1-4 A jumper being lowered to the ground after a jump.

It is also interesting that some insurance companies will not insure commercial site that offer water dunking, or similar stunts.

Hot Air Balloon

Tethered hot air balloons became popular as a bungee platform when authorities began stopping the use of bridges due to trespassing laws. At first, the FAA didn't concern themselves with the new fad because they believed it would be short-lived. That was not the case. So, in October of 1990, the FAA published a memo to its field inspectors, stating that no field approvals were to be given for balloons that were to be used as a bungee platform. A field approval is an inspection similar to the safety inspection on a car. If the balloon appears to be airworthy, the field inspector provides the balloon owner with a certificate of airworthiness. Without this certification, a balloon cannot operate legally.

Any modification to a balloon also requires an inspection. So, even balloons that had current airworthiness certifications had to have an inspection if they attached the bungee equipment to the balloon. The FAA's memo caused the balloon bungee sites to either shut down or to operate illegally. The fines for operating illegally could be as heavy as ten thousand dollars plus the revocation of the pilot's license.

In May of 1991, the FAA published another memo stating that any modification to the balloons for bungee jumping would be handled in the same manner as for modifications made for any other purpose. The balloonist requests an inspection by the field inspector, and he decides if the changes are minor enough that a simple additional field approval would suffice, or if an engineering data package showing the changes should be turned into the FAA for detailed review. If the FAA engineers decide that the modifications do not compromise the airworthiness of the balloon, an approval is given. The FAA has stressed that the bungee equipment is not being regulated, only the modifications made to the balloon. The modifications may be for the purpose of picking up pink elephants or for bungee jumping. That has no bearing on the approval process.

Commercial balloon bungee sites tether their hot air balloons. There are several reasons for this. It would be pretty tough to keep the balloon in the jump zone if it was not tied down. It would fly off every time it launched with a jumper. Then it would be difficult to land the balloon with the jumper dangling from the bottom. The jumper would be touching the ground, and the balloon would still be traveling, dragging the jumper along the ground. The poor jumper would be hitting trees, houses and power lines. The tether lines also provide double checks for better height control. Lastly, the FAA has regulations that prohibit the dangling of objects from a free-flying balloon, but not from a tethered balloon.

Many jumpers are concerned about the jolting of the hot air balloon when the jumper leaves the balloon and when the jumper changes directions during the jump. When the jumper jumps from the balloon, he removes his weight from the balloon's load. Then his weight is added to the balloon's load when he reaches the bottom of the fall. A second later, as he starts upward, his weight is subtracted from the load of the balloon. Since the time between the subtraction and addition of his weight is only a few seconds, the effect on the balloon is minimal.

It requires several minutes of pulling in the same direction to move the one ton balloon a substantial distance. The biggest movement is felt in the basket, as it is free to swing under the balloon as the jumper leaps outward. Even that movement is minimal, and the pilot is not in danger of falling out of the basket from the jolt. In most cases, the bungee cords are attached to the envelope cables. That means the heaviest part of the balloon is taking the brunt of the stress instead of the light-weight basket.

The acceleration of the jumper during his freefall does increase his velocity. A 100-foot fall increases his velocity by about three times. However, the additional force is mostly absorbed by the elasticity of the cords, and the balloon does not receive the impact of the total velocity in one intense jolt.

After the jumper is through bouncing around, it is very simple to return the jumper to the ground. He is swinging at a fairly consistent distance from the balloon, and the balloon is slowly lowered until the jumper touches the ground. The ground crew unhooks him from the cord and he walks away. The balloon, having the weight subtracted from its load, floats upward for a few seconds, then settles to the ground. The next jumper is hooked up and the balloon rises.

If the commercial site offers the option of dunking into water from a balloon, it is not a good idea at all to exercise that option. The balloon shifts downward when the jumper reaches the bottom of his fall. In addition, winds can cause sudden downshifts and can drive a balloon sideways clear across the jump zone away from the ideal dunking spot. The balloon is absolutely too unstable of a platform to be playing with no or little margin for error.

Crane

Many experienced jumps believe the crane produces the greatest thrill per feet of height. It has been stated that with a balloon, bridge or tower, the structure is bulky around the jumping ledge which makes the jumper feel cradled and protected. With a crane, there is very little hardware surrounding the jumping cage and the jumper feels like a bird in the top of a very wimpy tree. The height is felt more intensely.

The jumper jumps from a cage that hangs from the cable attached to the boom of the crane. The jumper enters the cage as it sets on the ground. He is hooked in with safety hooks since not much else holds him in the cage. The crane lifts the jumper to the desired height. Then the jump master unhooks the jumper and tells him to jump. After he completes his bounces, the crane lowers him back to the ground and the ground crew unhooks him. The cage returns to the ground to accept the next customer.

The crane seems to be a favorite platform for a stunt called a negative jump. Please note that the author thinks this stunt at a commercial site is about as stupid as the water dunking stunt. Please leave it to the stuntmen. The jump starts with the jumper on the ground. About ten people hold the jumper down as the crane pulls the cage upward, stretching the cord. Then when the cord is very taunt, all the people let go and the jumper zooms upwards toward the cage. (Figure 1-5)

The problem with this jump is that it is very difficult to judge how much energy is being stored in the cords, and it is unknown how far the jumper will be hurdled. That means it is very possible, in fact, sometimes it is the goal of the

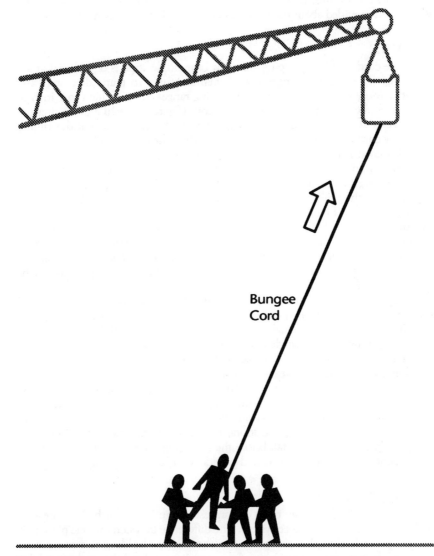

**Bungee
Cord**

Figure 1-5 Negative jump.

crew, to cause the jumper to go higher than the cage. That is okay as long as the jumper doesn't smack into the cage on the way up or on the way down. There is no guarantee what path the jumper will follow, or how high. The chances of hitting the cage is fairly high, too high for a commercial site.

Tower

It is challenging to provide specific information on towers since they can be so varied in structure, height, and the jumping methods used. Most of the information provided about the bridge can be applied to jumping from a tower.

CORDS

The cords used for jumping are made of multiple strands of rubber that are bound tightly together. Bungee cord is manufactured in many diameters and strengths. Most cord that is used for bungeeing ranges from 3/8 inch to 1 inch in diameter. Some bungee sites use only one cord (figure 1-6) while other sites use up to five or six cords bundled together (figure 1-7). The factor that determines how many cords are used is the breaking strength of the cord.

If a cord is designed to have a high breaking strength, fewer cords are required to handle the same jump as a greater number of cords with a lesser breaking strength. The most commonly used cord in the United States is a nylon or cotton sheathed military specification cord with a diameter of 5/8 inch and a breaking strength of more than 1000 pounds. Technically, one cord could handle the stress produced by a jumper weighing 150 pounds, which is roughly 450 pounds. However, that stress would cause the cord to stretch further than recommended by the manufacturer. Therefore, most bungee sites using military specification cords use one cord per every fifty pounds of the jumper's body weight to achieve the desired stretch.

In most countries other than the United States, the commonly used cord has a breaking strength easily capable of handling the stress created by a jump.

It is the author's personal opinion that a sheathed multiple cord system is better than an unsheathed single cord system. The arguments behind that opinion are as follows. Multiple cords allow each cord to act as part of a back-up system for the other cords. If one cord breaks, the remainder of the cords should still be intact and keep the jumper from falling to the ground. Instead, the jumper only drops a few additional feet but is then stopped. With a single cord system, there is no back-up.

Another reason is that the sheathing is a valuable accessory. Many cords are designed so that the sheathing is as strong as or stronger than the rubber. In testing, the rubber has a tendency to fail before the sheathing. The strength of the sheath complements the strength of rubber and provides an additional back-up.

HARNESSES

There are basically two types of harnesses. One is the full body harness. It can be a one piece or two piece system. The difference between the one piece and the two piece is that the one piece has short straps holding the two pieces together. The top piece is worn around the armpits and shoulders, and around the back to the front. It is put on as if it were a jacket. The bottom piece is worn around the tops of the thighs, and from the buttocks through the crotch and around the waist to join in the front. It is put on as if it were a pair of shorts. The bungee cord is attached in the front to both harnesses. (Figure 1-8)

There have been a few complaints about the discomfort felt by males at the bottom of the initial fall when there is stress on the harness. However, no serious or permanent injury seems to have arisen from this discomfort.

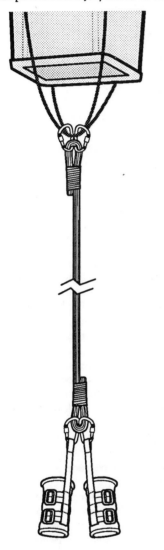
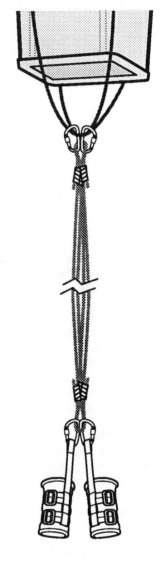

Figure 1-6 Single-cord bungee system.   **Figure 1-7** Multi-cord bungee system.

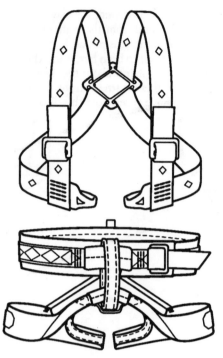

Figure 1-8 The two parts of the full-body harness.

The other type of harness is an ankle harness. Either both ankles can be attached or just one. Some ankle harnesses are a simple bracelet-looking affair that only cover a couple of inches of the ankle. The stress is mainly placed on the ankle. Other, better, harnesses cover the leg from ankle to knee and are held tight by velcro and double-back buckles. The stress is then placed on the entire lower leg. (Figure 1-9).

Relatively few questions arise about the full-body harness. The most concern seems to be about the ankle harnesses. Jumpers are worried that ankle harnesses could come off the ankle. The track record for these harnesses shows that this has not been a problem. After millions of jumps done world-wide, such an incident has not been recorded. The harnesses are attached so tightly that they would have a tough time coming off, even if the jumper's shoes came off.

Some experienced jumpers believe jumping with a full-body harness causes a greater thrill than jumping with ankle harnesses. Other retreads believe the opposite. It is a great debate for a boring Saturday evening.

With a full-body harness, jumpers have the freedom to jump head-first or feet-first, or to jump facing the platform or away from the platform. However, with ankle harnesses, it is normal to either do a swan dive or a back dive. Most commercial sites will instruct beginning jumpers on their preferred or required method of jumping. At the time the jumper has completed his bounces and is swinging, a full-body harness naturally places the jumper in a position as if he were sitting in a reclining chair. The natural position with the ankle harnesses is

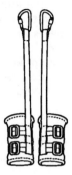

Figure 1-9 Ankle Harness

completely upside-down. That can be rather uncomfortable to have blood rush to the head for two or three minutes. It is also uncomfortable to land on the head. In order to avoid the discomfort some sites have devised methods of getting the jumper to an upright position. One common method is to attach a knotted rope along the bottom few feet of the cord. During one of the rebounds while the jumper is weightless, he pulls himself upright by "climbing" the knotted rope and tucks his feet under him in a kneeling position. Then he is kneeling during the last minute of the jump, and can stand up as he touches the earth. (Figure 1-10)

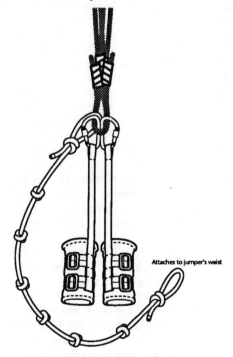

Attaches to jumper's waist

Figure 1-10 Knotted rope for returning to an upright position while wearing ankle harness.

Ankle harnesses have straps that attach the cords. The straps keep the jumper two or three feet away from the cords and carabiners. The straps are made of a very strong webbing that is stronger than the bungee cord.

The first few bottom feet of the cords are usually covered with some sort of padding, or bumper, that helps keep the jumper away from the cords and metal parts. This avoids "bungee kisses," or bruises, from getting hit by metal parts or the whipping bungee cord.

INDUSTRY PROFILE

It is difficult to compile statistics on the bungee industry because there is no tracking mechanism in place today. some tracking is being established, but estimations are still fairly rough.

To date, there are about 500 sites world wide in the United States, New Zealand, Australia, France, Germany, Norway, Canada and South Africa. There are about 150 sites in the United States. The state that has the most sites is California, the first on opened in 1989.

States that started sites in 1990 are mostly costal states, Inland states are blooming in 1991.

There have been about three million jumps made in the world. In the United States, there have been about a half-million jumps made through legitimate sites and maybe more than that made by covert jumping sites. Bungee jumping has an extremely low fatality/injury rate considering the number of jumps logged. In France, three people died in 1989. A former Miss Australia broke her collarbone in 1990 during a tandem (two person) jump. In 1990, a United States stuntman jumped from a billboard without calculating the cord's stretch and broke his back.

In 1991, the number of commercial sites skyrocketed and yet the statistics remained relatively the same. A United States man sustained severe pelvic injuries when he came too close to the ground while attempting to pick up a soda can from an earth-bound person's hand after jumping from a hot air balloon tethered at ninety-six feet. He was an employee performing a stunt for the customers. A teen-age girl in South Africa fell to her death when one of the straps that held the cord to her ankle harness broke. A man in Norway feel to belly-flop into deep water when his cord broke. He sustained serious injury In the United States, a bungee instructor forgot to hook up the bottom half of his full-body harness. As he was demonstrating to his class, his harness fell off and he fell about sixty-five feet to his death.

In the early days of bungee jumping, it was generally believed that the fad would be short-lived. That has not been the case. It is still growing. Commercial sites are showing up at a rapid rate. For example in the United States, there were about twenty-five commercial sites in operation at the end of 1990. A year later, there were more than 150 sites in operation. Educated guessers have estimated that the United States will have as many as 500 sites within two years. The industry will eventually saturate the market, and the business will not be profitable due to the lack of first-time thrill seekers.

Chapter Summary

Introduction

- Bungee jumping is the sport of jumping, while attached to elastic cords, from a high platform.
- BASE jumping is different than bungee jumping.
- The jot that a jumper experiences is not as severe as it appears to an earth-bound spectator.
- During the training, a site should include an explanation of what is expected of the customer, and what can be expected of the site operators. Waiver forms may be produced for signatures.
- The time from when the jumper leaves the ground for the ride up to the jumping height until his feet are back on the ground can be anywhere from two to fifteen minutes.
- Generally, the height of commercial jumping platforms ranges from fifty feet to three hundred feet.

History

- Legend has it that bungee jumping first came into being on the Pentecost Island in the New Hebrides of the South Pacific.
- Modern day bungee jumping was born on April Fools' Day 1979 when the Oxford Dangerous Sports Club of Britain attached themselves to bungee cords and leaped off the 245-foot Clifton Bridge in Bristol England.
- Commercial bungee sites started appearing around 1986 in various European countries. The first commercial site in the United States began business in 1989.

Platforms—Bridge

- Bridges were initially the favored platform because they required the least preparation and were plentiful.
- At this time in the United States, it is illegal to jump from most public bridges.
- Basically there are two ways to get the jumper off the cord, take him up or take him down.

Platforms—Hot air balloons

- In May of 1991, the FAA published a memo stating that any modification to the balloons for bungee jumping would be handled in the same manner as modifications made for any other purpose.
- Many jumpers are concerned about the jolting of the hot air balloon when the jumper leaves the balloon and when the jumper changes directions during the jump.
- After a jump, the pilot lowers the balloon and jumper to the ground.
- Dunking jumpers into water from a balloon is not a good idea.

Crane

- Cranes are currently the platform of choice from the commercial standpoint.
- The negative jump is a popular jump from the crane, but is not a safe type of jump.

Tower

- The term "tower" usually means any stationary platform that isn't a bridge, crane, or hot air balloon.

- The design and size of towers vary greatly.

Cords
- The cords used for jumping are made of multiple strands of rubber that are bound tightly together and are manufactured in many thicknesses and strengths.
- If a cord is designed to have a high breaking strength, fewer cords are required to handle the same jump as a greater number of cords with a lesser breaking strength.
- The most commonly used cords in the United States are a military specification cord.
- It is the author's personal opinion that a sheathed multiple cord system is better than an unsheathed single cord system.
- There are basically two types of harnesses, the full body harness and the ankle harness.

Industry Profile
- To date, there are about 500 sites world wide, about 150 sites in the United States.
- There have been about three million jumps made in the world.
- Bungee jumping has an extremely low fatality/injury rate considering the number of jumps logged.
- Commercial sites are showing up at a rapid rate.

CHAPTER TWO

How to be an Informed Customer

W ith all of the technical information related to bungee jumping, it seems impossible to know just enough to pick a quality site without having an engineering degree. Relax, it is possible. This chapter covers many issues that a potential commercial site customer would consider in making an educated choice.

FINDING POTENTIAL SITES

There are several ways to find the nearest commercial bungee sites. One way is to contact a bungee association. Refer to Chapter 17 for further information on the various associations. Sports writers for local newspapers or skydiving enthusiasts may be aware of the closest sites. The telephone directory may have a listing under "bungee". A site located in another state may know of a nearby site. A little bit of homework should turn up at least one potential site.

Price

Of course, the price will vary with each site. A state where there are many sites, such as California, the competition will have brought the price down in comparison with the rest of the United States. If a site is the only site within five hundred miles, it can pretty well name its own price because people will pay dearly for that once-in-a-lifetime thrill.

Another factor is the site owner's overhead expense. If the site owner is jumping from a bridge and has no insurance, he basically pays for his cords and hired help. If a site owner paid cash for an eighty thousand dollar crane and pays fifteen percent of gross for insurance, plus provides workman's compensation (as required) for his hired help, and in addition, makes sure his equipment is top quality and in top shape, his overhead eats most of his profits. He has to charge a substantial fee to stay in business.

One amusement park offers jumps from a 75-foot tower for $15 to $25 a jump, in addition to the amusement park entrance fee. A California crane site offers two jumps from 150 feet for $130. Other sites ask $99 for crane jumps from 200 feet.

Sometimes a site will include a complimentary video of the customer jumping, or a tee-shirt, with the first jump. Subsequent jumps with the same site may be provided for a smaller price. Many sites offer group rates if one person acts as a point of contact for the rest of the group. That lessens the number of phone calls for the site's jump coordinator. Advance payment, or at least a reservation fee, is usually required. Each site has their own policy on this, and on cancellation fees. It is important to know the details about these fees to avoid surprises later.

Making the Appointment

Since many sites require a reservation as much as a month in advance, it is wise to plan way ahead. If a site only takes walk-ons, the customer can find out what are the busy days and hours and avoid them. The average wait in line may be important information also.

The customer needs to find out if training is required, how much time is involved in the training, and if it is the same day as the jump. He should ask what type of clothing is needed. Directions to the site or office are nice to have.

Due to changes that have to be made to the equipment as different size people jump, most sites have limits on weight and size. A common weight limit is 250 pounds, and the jumper needs to be able to fit into the harnesses securely. Again, check with the individual site.

Some sites allow minors to jump if a parent signs a release form, other sites won't allow minors to jump under any circumstance. The intense regulations concerning insurance and liability force site owners to be sticklers about this issue.

When a jumper arrives at the site to make a jump, the site owners assume that the jumper is responsible enough to refrain from jumping if he has a health problem that could cause trouble during the jump. In a waiver form, there is usually a clause to that effect that the jumper is required to sign. The type of health problems that can cause trouble include, but are not limited to, neck, back, hip, blood pressure and heart problems. Please realize that this type of activity causes adrenaline to race through the body in massive quantities. The jumper's heart beats super fast, blood pressure increases, breathing is irregular, all the fear reflexes kick in. There is some stress to the muscles and joints. A person with epilepsy or who is pregnant could suffer problems.

It is a temptation to calm the intense anxiety during the hours preceding the jump by drinking alcohol or taking in some controlled substance. Again, due to liability concerns, if a jumper appears to be under the influence of some substance, most sites will promptly ask the jumper to leave the site. This probably means the jump, and the money paid for it, will be forfeited.

Insurance/Waivers

Some sites will require the jumper to sign a waiver that states the jumper is aware that he is about to take part in a dangerous sport, that he understands the risks, and that he will not hold the site responsible for any injury resulting from the jump. If a customer has a problem with signing such a waiver, the conflict needs to be settled before the customer places any money down. The day of the jump is not the best day to hound the ground crew about such technicalities.

The customer should find out, in advance, if the site has insurance that would cover the jumper in the case of an accident. The insurance that is usually carried only covers the site should the jumper sue the site owner and win. If the jumper has signed a waiver, the chances of winning a court case is slim, unless the customer can prove that the site was negligent in their operation.

However, recently some insurance companies have been offering a supplemental policy for the jumpers. It is offered for an additional few dollars. With this policy, the jumper is covered if he sustains an injury during the jump. The coverage is small, maybe as little as ten thousand dollars. Yet, if the jumper broke his arm, the treatment probably would not run more than that amount. The jumper would be covered without having to sue the site. This is still a new option, and not many sites have taken advantage of the option, so the customer needs to ask specific questions to confirm it is this policy and not just a liability policy.

The reason the above policy has come into being is because many personal health plans don't cover a person if they are injured while participating in a high-risk sport. Unfortunately, bungee jumping is often placed in that category. The jumper should contact his personal health policy carrier to find if he will be covered during the jump.

Judging the Quality of a Site

The jumper may wish to view the site prior to the day of his jump. This will provide him with an idea of what to expect. He can watch the actions of the crew while his brain is free of extreme anxiety. He can see what level of skill is required of the jumpers. Of course, this allows him to laugh at the strange actions of the jumpers as they let go of the platform. Watching other jumpers tends to build the confidence level of a jumper-to-be. There is something contagious about watching jumper after jumper get super-charged with adrenaline and then whoop and holler and slap other jumpers on the back with intense comraderie. It also makes the unknown a little less unknown.

If a site is reluctant to allow a jumper-to-be to visit the site prior to his jump, it may be a clue that there is a valid concern about the quality of the site. It would be a good time to ask some pointed questions and uncover the "why's". The customer is putting his money and his life on the line, and he has every right to know about anything that concerns his safety.

While every site has their equipment set up differently, there are some consistent indications of a quality site. A site might only follow one or two of these guidelines and still be a high quality site. Therefore, the following is like a spot check. Think of each compliance as a brownie point. If a site does not comply with one of the guidelines, it could be grounds for an investigative question.

Each link of the bungee system should be redundant (Figure 2-1). This means that there should be more than one cord used. The cords could be attached to the harness with only one carabiner, but two carabiners allow for a back-up should one be faulty. If each bungee cord is attached independently to the platform, it is not deadly if the carabiner holding one of the cords fails. If the two ankle harnesses are attached separately to the bungee cords, the jumper won't fall if one of the harnesses comes unattached. It is smart to have a back-up seat harness when the jumper is using ankle harnesses.

Ideally, a jumper should not come very close to the ground during his jump. But, the bungee novice is going to have trouble knowing how close is too close. A good formula is to take the height of the jumping platform and divide that distance by four. A jumper should not come closer to the ground than the distance equal to one fourth of the platform height. If the platform is three hundred feet high, the jumper should always be at least seventy five feet above the ground during the jump (Figure 2-2). This allows a margin for the variations in the distance fallen due to air temperature, body weights, styles of jumps, age of the cord and other factors such the shifting of a hot air balloon.

The breaking strength of the set of cords used should have a safety margin of at least five times the force applied. That means that the cords are designed to handle stress equal to five times the amount of stress to which they are being subjected. A simple formula for figuring the stress the cords are being subjected to is to multiply the jumper's weight by three. A person weighing 150 pounds causes a stress of about 450 pounds. Therefore, the set of cords should collectively have a breaking strength of at least 2,250 pounds. Any crew member should know the collective breaking strength of the set of cords being used at the site.

A site can go overboard in the use of safety equipment, but who is to say how much is too much? Helmets can prevent a concussion if the jumper hits the jump ledge on the way down. Gloves can prevent rope and cord burns, which can be severe enough to remove large patches of skin. It is easy to get fingers in between the metal rings, which gloves could lessen the impact of that contact. Goggles can help avoid the sting of running into a beetle with the eyeball at forty miles-per-hour. A few feet of non-stretchable webbing can keep the jumper away from the snapping, expanding, burning bungee cord. A padded bumper wrapped

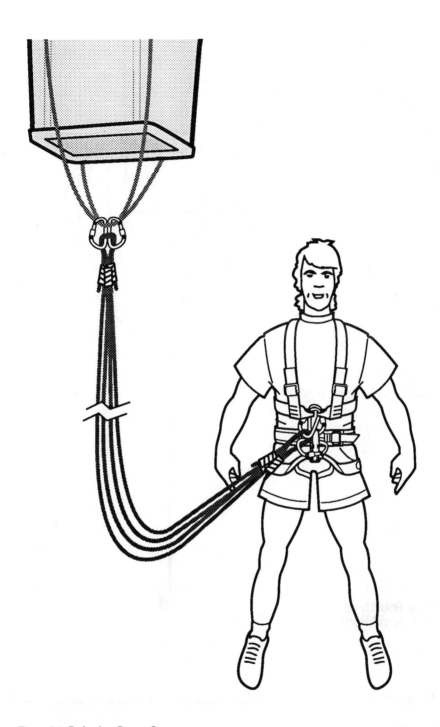

Figure 2-1 Redundant Bungee System

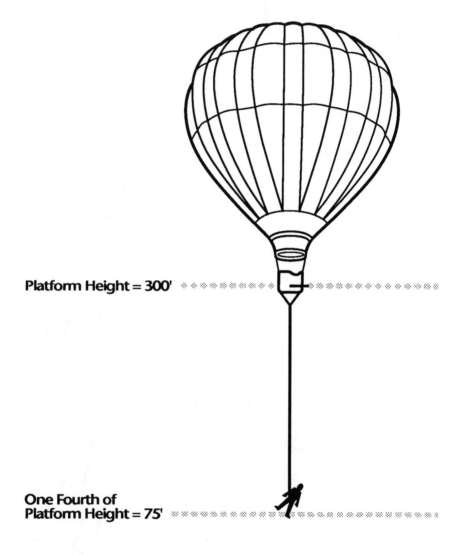

Platform Height = 300'

One Fourth of Platform Height = 75'

Ground

Figure 2-2 Distance jumper should remain from ground.

around the bottom few feet of the bungee cord softens the blow to the jumpers head as he meets the hard cords.

If an accident should occur, the crew members should be well-versed in how to react. It should be known in advance who would call for an ambulance, and where the nearest phone is located. It is recommended that there be at least one crew member on duty at all times who has been professionally trained in first-aid. Even more desirable would be for that crew member to be certified as an Emergency Medical Technician or Paramedic. It is ideal to have backboards, splints, bandages, and other first-aid equipment at the site.

Covered, or sheathed cords tend to have a better track record for staying in one piece as the cord whips around. Unsheathed cords have been known to fall apart while partially relaxed.

The site's operation should run smoothly. Each crew member should know his job thoroughly, and should perform it without prompting. If a crew member is to catch the hot air balloon as it lands, he should be there every time, unfailing. There should not be last-minute instructions to the crew delivered via a harried shout. The person putting harnesses on the customers should be practiced and proficient, and be able to answer any question about the harness knowledgeably. The crew should have excellent crowd and customer control, keeping the crowd out of the jump zone.

If the site offers specialties such as negative jumps (see Figure 1-5, page 14), tandem jumps (two people secured together), or head dunks into water, it may be an indication that they are more interested in making a few extra bucks than in the safety of their customers. Each of those specialties removes some safety factors, and require super careful calculations and a special environment. That is not to say that a site that offers these jumps is not a quality site, but again, it might be a good time for investigative questioning.

Some sites state that they are a member of an association. While a positive sign, it does not necessarily mean that they meet any certain guidelines or standards. At this time, there is not a wide-spread method of certifying a site. Each association, each insurance company, each franchise has their own set of guidelines. It is anticipated that in the near future national guidelines will be developed and widely used. Until that point, be aware of the situation.

A commercial bungee site is a business just as is a grocery store, and is subject to the laws governing the operation of a business. A site owner can run an operation that looks top notch on the surface, but yet may be operating illegally. That means that the may not really have insurance, they may not have business permits, they may not be paying commercial taxes, they may not even be a registered entity. A quick call to City Hall can reveal whether they are operating according to the law. Even if they are based in another area, they should have operating permits for the area. If they are not a "legal" site, it may mean that the customer's rights are not being protected, and that is reason for concern.

Chapter Summary:
  Finding Potential Sites:
  • There are several ways to find the nearest commercial bungee sites.

Price:
- The price of jumps can range from $15 to $130, and may include more than one jump or souvenirs.

Making the Appointment:
- Since many sites require a reservation as much as a month in advance, it is wise to plan way ahead.
- Most sites have limits on weight and size.
- The site owner expects the customer to refrain from jumping if the jumper has serious health problems.
- A jumper may forfeit his jump if he is under the influence of drugs or alcohol.

Insurance/Waivers:
- Some sites will require the jumper to sign a waiver.
- Many personal health plans don't cover a person if they are injured while participating in a high-risk sport; however, a few sites offer a supplemental medical policy to cover a jumper during a jump.

Judging the Quality of a Site:
- Each link of the bungee system should be redundant.
- Ideally, a jumper should not come very close to the ground during his jump.
- The breaking strength of the set of cords used should have a safety margin of at least five times the force applied.
- The use of personal safety equipment protects the crew and jumpers.
- If an accident should occur, the crew members should be well-versed in how to react.
- The site's operation should run smoothly.
- If the site offers special jumps, it may be an indication that they are more interested in making a few extra bucks than in the safety of their customers.
- Bungee sites are a profit organization and are subject to local business regulations.

CHAPTER THREE

Using a Bridge as a Jumping Platform

As mentioned earlier, bridges are a readily available bungee jumping platform. They require no assembly, they are picture pretty, they provide awesome views, and they are the traditional bungee platform. There are short bridges, tall bridges, skinny bridges, wide bridges, muscular bridges, lacy bridges, and practical bridges. However, the problem lies with finding a bridge from which bungee jumping is legal.

LEGALITIES

In many countries other than the United States, bridge bungee jumping is allowed. In the United States, the story is different. In most cases, it is outright illegal to bungee jump from a bridge in the United States, end of argument. However, two states have no laws that make bungeeing illegal. Those two states are Washington and Oregon. Bridge bungee jumping has blossomed there, as expected. That is beautiful country, and they have some exquisite bridges.

In all other states, jumping from government-owned bridges constitutes trespassing, and that is a crime. Railroad companies have a tendency to press charges on people jumping from their railroad bridges. Fair enough, since the railroad company could be held liable in the case of an injury or death.

Should a jumper be charged with trespassing, he is subject to time in jail and a steep fine. Some locations have fines as steep as one thousand dollars. The government, and railroad companies have been known to sue covert bridge bungee sites for an amount equal to the company's gross income, and for taxes on unreported income. That is a nasty penalty!

It is possible to set up a legitimate, legal bridge site in the United States in states other than Washington and Oregon. A bridge can be bought, leased, borrowed with permission, or built. Considerable footwork is required to find a bridge with potential. To find a bridge that has the desired qualities in such areas as height, side-to-side clearance, appearance and accessibility, the site-owner-to-be has to do some driving in the country, hound real estate offices, search in encyclopedias, follow railroad tracks or float down rivers. After the bridge is found, the person has to figure out who owns the bridge. The local courthouse will be a great place to start digging for that information. If the government owns the bridge, or if the bridge is a railroad bridge that is currently being used, chances of successfully purchasing, leasing, or obtaining permission to use the bridge are slim. However, if the bridge is an abandoned highway or railroad, and is still in stable condition, then the chances are better.

When the person believes he has a bridge that may be a solid potential jump site, he needs to pull together a proposal. The proposal needs to prove that the venture will be financially profitable enough to support payments for the purchase/lease of the bridge. In the case of a lease or permission for use, the proposal needs to show that the bridge owner, and the owner of the land around the bridge, would not be liable in the event of an injury or death. The task of figuring out that detail belongs to a lawyer. The proposal should show that the bungee venture would not conflict with any local or state zoning or commercial regulations. Information on what exactly would be done at the site, and statistics on the safety of the sport should be provided in the proposal.

Then the site-owner-to-be goes for the gusto. It is very tough to work out a way to be able to bungee legally from a bridge—but, not impossible.

It is important to remember that any commercial venture, whether it is operated from a bridge or from a downtown office, is a business. This means that business permits are required, zoning regulations have to be followed, and taxes have to be paid. City Hall will be happy to provide the details.

SELECTING A BRIDGE

The neat part about bridges is that they are built at all different heights. A fifty foot bridge would make an ideal platform for first-time jumpers who are leery of extreme heights. On the other hand, a five hundred foot bridge would be too high for most site customers, and the demand probably would not support the investment. A bridge that high is great for competition and the ultra-daring experienced jumper. A two hundred foot bridge would probably draw a substantial flow of customers.

Since a bridge that is available for legal jumping is difficult to find, the person probably is not going to have much choice on whether the bridge is over land or water. However, if the person has a choice, there are a few considerations. In the unfortunate event that a jumper is accidentally dropped to the ground, his chances could be increased by landing in water vice on dry land. Yet, if the jumper does hit the water, it may be too shallow to really make a difference, or he may hit rocks or floating debris.

If the site owner decides to lower his customers after the jump and his bridge is over water, he has to figure out how to keep the jumpers dry. He could lower them into a boat. That requires extra manpower, presents the chance of flipping the boat, and is more time consuming than lowering them to dry land.

Some marketing whizzes figure that a bridge near a well-traveled highway would provide free advertising. True. However, there are a few problems with that idea. When a motorist who is driving down the road enveloped in his personal thoughts suddenly sees, out of the corner of his eye, a person jump off of a high bridge, he tends to slam on the brakes and drive in the ditch. This tends to cause accidents. The highway patrol tend to get irate at the rash of accidents. The highway patrol has ways of getting a site shut down by claiming it is a traffic hazard.

Being near a well-traveled road also draws the crowds, which can be desirable. That is, as long as the crowds don't cause traffic hazards with their illegal parking and U-turns in strange places.

There are relatively few structural criteria for a bridge that is to be used for bungee jumping. It needs to be structurally sound. The area to which the bungee equipment will be attached should be able to support the weight of the equipment and the stress of the jolts. It doesn't have to possess any special poles, bumps, lips or hooks for attaching the equipment. Clever engineering will allow the attachment of the bungee equipment to just about any structural design.

There needs to be a side-to-side clearance under the bridge sufficient for the movements of the jumper. The side-to-side clearance should be equal to 150% of relaxed cord length or 75% of extended cord length.3 If the bridge is 200 feet high and the jumper wishes to fall 150 feet, the relaxed cord should equal 75 feet and expand to 150 feet. The side-to-side clearance should be at least 113 feet in any direction. (Figure 3-1)

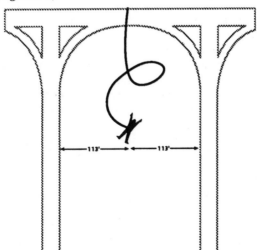

Figure 3-1 Side-to-side clearance.

OPERATIONAL ISSUES

The bridge presents an interesting dilemma when it comes to retrieving the bungeeist at the completion of his jump. The logistics of the retrieval system have to be worked out on a case-by-case basis. Every bridge will be different, every bungee system will be different, each site owner will have different ideas, and the system integration engineer will have his own theories. However, following are a few generic grains of food for thought.

The first challenge is to figure out whether to raise or lower the jumper to retrieve him. If the jumper is raised back to the top of the bridge, extra power is required to counteract gravity. One way to accomplish that is to attach a rope to the jumper and then run the rope through a pulley mounted on the edge of the bridge. A group of people on the top of the bridge pull on the rope and raise the jumper to the top. Another possibility is to have a motorized pulley system mounted on the edge of the bridge.

An advantage to raising the jumper rather than lowering him is that if the pulley system were to fail, the jumper is still attached to the bungee cord and would simply fall back onto the bungee cords.

If the jumper is lowered, that back-up system is taken away. The bungee cords have to be disconnected either from the jumper or from the bridge. That is, unless the length of the cords can be adjusted. That could be done if the cords were on a spool. A system like that requires extra careful engineering to avoid costly mistakes.

Due to cooperation with gravity, less effort is required to lower the jumper to the ground than to raise him. However, if the bridge is over water, extra crew members are needed to man a boat and make sure the jumper gets to dry land safely. If the water is a fast moving river, it may be dangerous to try to land the jumper in the boat and to maneuver the boat in the current.

Whether the retrieval system is designed to raise or lower the jumper, it is important that the pulley system is not attached to the jumper or the bungee system during the jump since the rope may get tangled in the cords. Also, the pulley wheels may be damaged or knocked loose if they are subjected to repeated jolts from the bounces.

Another challenge is getting the retrieval rope to the jumper as he is dangling on the cord. The rope cannot be tied along the length of the cord during the jump because the rope won't stretch nearly as much as the cord will. The rope can't be hanging loose near the jumper during the jump since the jumper or the cord could tangle with the rope. It is difficult to lower a rope to the jumper and get it close enough for him to grab.

One idea is to tie a carabiner to the end of the rope and then close the carabiner around the top of the bungee cord. The carabiner will slide down the cord to the jumper. (Figure 3-2) He then can hook the carabiner to his harness to prepare for the ride.

Night jumping is a unique experience, but the question is raised about the special problems involved. First, some states have bungee regulations or amusement regulations that require special lighting and other safety enhancements. Other concerns include the ability of the crew to see problems with the cords, such as tangles or failing connections. If the jumper will be

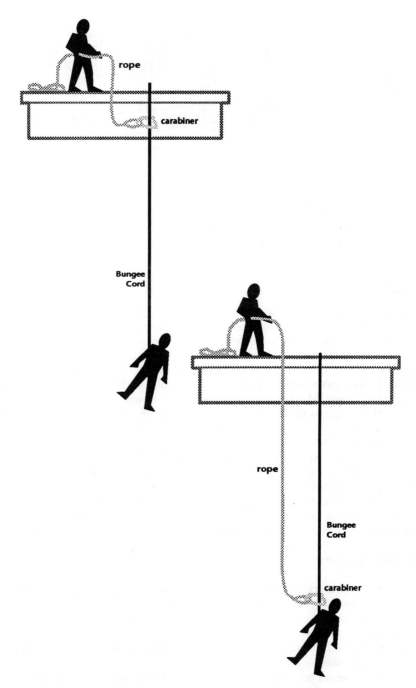

Figure 3-2 Sending retrieval rope to jumper.

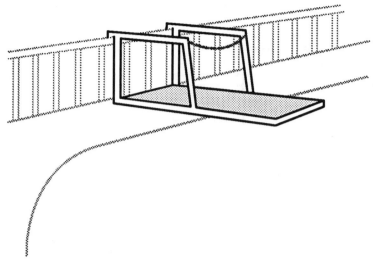

Figure 3-3 Bridge jumping shelf.

lowered into water, the crew may have trouble navigating the boat or landing the jumper. The customers or onlookers may trip over a rock. A lighting system can lessen or resolve some of the problems.

While a jumping shelf is not necessary, it is recommended. Most bridges have some type of railing, and if a jumper has to stand or sit on the railing to jump, he may loose his footing, or be uncomfortable with his footing. He may hit the railing or the side of the bridge as he leaps. A jumping shelf helps the jumper get further out from the bridge. (Figure 3-3) It is vital that the shelf be attached securely to the bridge. Otherwise, the poor jumper may jump a little sooner than expected, which just might not be funny.

The shelf could be as small as a two-by-two foot platform, or could be a diving board with a little spring. It is wise to have some kind of railing and a safety gate, even a thin cable railing is better than nothing.

As for attaching the bungee system to the bridge, that has to be specially designed for the type of equipment and type of bridge. The bungee system manufacture usually will provide guidelines for attaching the system.

Chapter Summary:

Legalities:
- In most states, jumping from government-owned bridges constitutes trespassing; however, a bridge can be bought, leased, borrowed with permission, or built.

Selecting a Bridge:
- A two hundred foot bridge would probably draw a substantial flow of customers.
- There are pros and cons to a bridge standing over water and to a bridge near a well-traveled road.

- There needs to be a side-to-side clearance under the bridge sufficient for the movements of the jumper.

Operational Issues:
- The logistics of the retrieval system have to be worked out on a case-by-case basis.
- One challenge is getting the retrieval rope to the jumper as he is dangling on the cord.
- Night jumping is a unique experience, but there are special problems involved.
- While a jumping shelf is not necessary, it is recommended.

CHAPTER FOUR

Using a Hot Air Balloon as a Jumping Platform

Hot air balloons are graceful and fascinating. They provide a vibrant color-filled backdrop for a swan dive bungee jump. During the first months after authorities began cracking down on bungeeing from bridges, hot air balloons became the salvation of the industry. Following are some of issues concerning hot air balloons and the bungee sport.

LEGALITIES

When hot air balloons were first used for bungee jumping, the FAA decided that it was only a minor concern because bungee jumping was a little-known fad that was going to pass quickly and without incident. However, that didn't happen. More than a few bungeeists turned to the hot air balloon when authorities started stifling the use of bridges for the sport. The FAA became concerned that if someone was killed or seriously injured, they would be blamed for not regulating an activity that is argumentatively within their jurisdiction.

In October of 1990, a memorandum was sent to all Regional Flight Standards Division Managers from the Acting Director of Flight Standards Service. (Appendix A) The memo instructed that any type of airworthiness or operational approval should not be issued for any product modified to incorporate bungee jumping operations. Furthermore, consideration had been given to shutting down bungee jumping sites that were already conducting business. FAA considered those sites to be operating in violation of Federal Aviation Regulations (FARs) 91.13 and 91.407. FAR 91.13 deals with the careless and reckless use of a certified aircraft and FAR 91.407 prohibits alterations or modifications to a certified aircraft without FAA approval.[4]

After several months of research and debate, the FAA published a second memo in May of 1991. (Appendix B) This memo gave guidance to field inspectors who were responsible for certifying the airworthiness of a balloon. They were instructed to handle the requests for approval of modifications to the balloons for bungee jumping as they would for modifications for any other purpose.

When a balloonist makes modifications to his balloon, he contacts his local certification office. There are certification offices in most major cities. He requests that a field inspector visit his site and review the modifications. The field inspector looks at the modifications, and using a reference manual put out by the FAA, he determines if the modifications need to be reviewed further by FAA engineers. If not, the inspector can sign a Form 337 immediately. This form is a two page form that verifies he reviewed and approved the modifications.

If the modifications are more complex, the inspector can request the balloonist to apply for either an engineering letter of approval, or a Supplemental Type Certificate (STC). The two documents are very close in nature, only the STC requires the compilation of a more formal engineering data package than the engineering letter of approval, and takes more time to process. To apply for either document, the balloonist compiles an information package showing details about the changes. The information is reviewed by an FAA engineer. If the engineer decides that the airworthiness of the balloon has not been compromised by the modifications, he will recommend approval. Then the balloonist will receive the document for which he applied.

Minor modifications are considered to be such changes as attaching carabiners that support the cords to tether points, or hanging a jumping shelf on the edge of the basket. Major modifications include drilling holes, cutting any part of the basket, or bolting on a platform to the basket.

If a balloonist flies his modified balloon without the modifications being approved by the FAA, he can be fined, and the pilot's license can be revoked.

Some balloon bungee sites got around all the above process by decertifying their balloon. Before a balloon can fly legally, a field inspector has to deem the balloon airworthy, and provide the balloon with a Type Certification. This is similar to a car's safety inspection. When modifications are made to the balloon, the Type Certification is voided until the modifications are approved.

If a balloon is not certified in the first place, there is no certification to be voided. That means the modifications do not have to be approved. FAR 101 allows a balloon to operate in a decertified state as long as the balloon is tethered only, never flown free. A decertified, tethered balloon is considered to be a moored aircraft. There are several restrictions concerning the use of a moored aircraft that are provided in the FAA's book of FARs.

The danger with encouraging bungeeists to use this option is that few balloonists are going to ground their perfectly airworthy balloon in order to use it for a few hours a day as a bungee platform. Therefore, it is a temptation to use old, unairworthy balloons that can't be certified anyway. That puts the bungee customers in extra danger.

Some bungee jumping has been done from free flying balloons. However, when a balloon is being used for bungee jumping, it should be tethered. The FAA considers bungee jumping from a free flying balloon to be careless and reckless use of the balloon and can punish the offender. Not only that, landing the balloon with a jumper hanging from the bottom would be a little rough on the jumper. The poor person would be hitting all the trees and power lines for quite a distance.

There is a rumor flying about that a tethered balloon does not have to flown by a licensed pilot. That is not the case. If the balloon is a certified aircraft, it has to be piloted by a licensed pilot. Furthermore, if it is being used as a commercial bungee platform, the pilot is required to have a commercial license.

When the site-owner-to-be begins the process of obtaining business permits and other required documents, he will more than likely be told that his business is considered to be an amusement. Usually the zoning requirements for such a venture are pretty extensive. It is worthwhile to argue to point that if a balloonist provided tethered balloon rides, the business would not be considered an amusement and that bungee jumping is really a glorified form of tethered balloon rides. It may not fly with the local zoning board, but it is worth the try. Another point of argument is that the bungee site is mobile and only stays set up for a few hours at a time, and usually only for a few months of the year.

SELECTING A HOT AIR BALLOON

Balloonists refer to the size of their balloon by an "AX" number. The balloon sizes that are most popular for bungee jumping are AX7, AX8, and AX9. The AX6 balloon seems to be too small to handle the quick changes in weight involved in bungeeing. The changes make the balloon bounce around and that could put the jumper and pilot in danger. An AX7 or 8 are nice and solid during a bungee jump. An AX9 is indeed stable enough for the job, but it requires quite a bit more propane and time to move it up and down. Since the balloon is raised and lowered repeatedly during bungee jumping, it can get expensive to heat up that large of a balloon over and over. Also, it takes more time for an AX9 to cool down and return to the ground than it does for an AX7, and that time means profit loss in a commercial operation.

It is difficult to recommend any particular make of balloon because each bungee-balloonist will swear by the make they fly. However, the balloonist has to figure out how to attach the bungee cords, and it seems logical to choose a balloon that will make that challenge easier.

The less stress that is carried by the basket, the better. If the bungee cords are attached directly to some part of the basket, the pilot is going to get a wild ride every time the jumper's weight is added and subtracted to and from the load. It is best to attach the load of the jumper to the envelope cables. Those

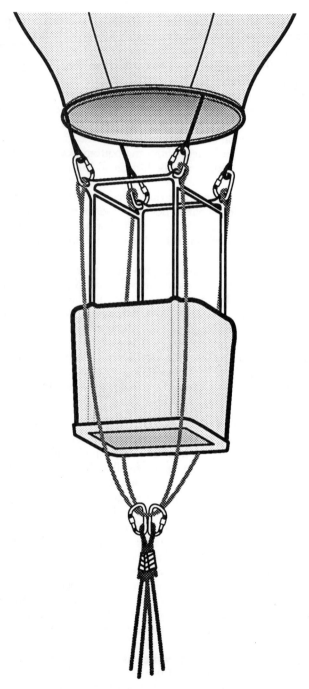

Figure 4-1 Attaching load of bungee cords to envelope cables and attachment points.

cables are designed to handle the passenger load. The envelope will be reluctant to move in response to the quick changes in the load. (Figure 4-1)

If it is not possible to attach directly to the cables, the next best option is to attach to some other load bearing point. Whatever point is chosen, make sure that point is designed to handle omnidirectional stress. Some pins and carabiners are weak when stressed in certain directions. Pay attention to the tether points, they usually are designed to handle omnidirectional stress.

The price range for balloons is as wide as it is for automobiles. The bottom of the range starts around ten thousand dollars. Higher durability, leather-covered poles, larger baskets, custom-designed envelopes, and larger envelopes all push the price up. Middle-of-the-line balloons run about forty or fifty thousand. It goes up from there to the very classy balloons.

In addition to the balloon, the accessories can cost a pretty penny. Fans, trailers and radios are an expensive necessary part of owning a balloon. The upkeep and repairs don't come cheap either.

OPERATIONAL ISSUES

Balloons are very limited in their times of operation. They can be flown at sunrise and sunset. In the winter, those hours usually can be extended since the air tends to be calmer. If there is more than just a slight breeze, or if there is rain or snow, the balloon cannot be flown. Since tethering is a touchier operation than free flying, the times of tethering are more scarce than those of free flying.

Tethering is touchier than free flying because when a balloon is flying free, it is moving with the air currents. When a balloon is tied down, it is forced to stand still as wind pushes against the envelope. It can be interesting to keep a balloon steady as weather cells hit, one after another, some warm and some cool. It is recommended that the pilot for a bungee balloon site has extensive experience at tethering. There is enough to worry about during a normal tether, and even more to worry about when a jumper is hanging from the bottom of the balloon.

A controversial issue is about the required number of tether ropes. Some pilots say that one tether point provides for optimal bungee operation, and other pilots say that the safest tether is with three ropes. One tether point allows the balloon the flow with the air currents, and is easier on the balloon as well as allows for the most relaxed tether. Three tether points keep the balloon where it is suppose to be, and controls the amount of running the ground crew has to do to do their jobs. Some pilots say that a scoop can help with the control of the balloon. A scoop is a panel attached at the bottom opening of the envelope to assist with wind control. An experienced pilot can determine the best set-up for the specific conditions.

Vehicles are common tether anchors. In bungee jumping, the vehicles are sometimes used to force the balloon back to the ground quicker than it would come down on its own. The vehicle drives away from the balloon. This pulls on the tether line attached to the vehicle that forces the balloon down.

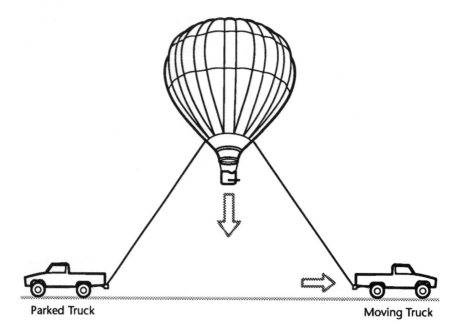

Parked Truck

Moving Truck

Figure 4-2 Vehicle forcing balloon to the ground.

(Figure 4-2) Forcing the balloon to lower puts extra stress on the tether points and could cause excess wear and tear on the attachment points. However, there is not information available on the results of the extra stress.

When using vehicles as anchors, it is important to remember that a gust of wind can move a balloon with enough force to drag several vehicles across the ground.

A danger that is present with a balloon that is not an issue with other types of platforms is the threat of fire. Due to the struggle between the tether lines and the wind controlling the movement of the balloon, the envelope tends to lean and fold in on itself. That can place the envelope line with the flame or the heat from the flame. This can cause the envelope to catch on fire.

As mentioned previously, balloons are limited in their times of the day of operation, as well as by weather and seasons. In southern states, an area with excellent wind patterns can plan on flying during as many as ninety percent of the sunrise and sunsets, year-around. Northern sites will have problems convincing customers and crew to show up during cold weather, which may limit the jumping season to four to eight months of the year. If a balloon site is set up in an area with poor wind patterns, the proforma can drop to thirty or forty percent, even in during the favorable months. Rainy/snowy climates will have a consistently lower proformance rate, also.

The land area required to operate a balloon bungee site varies with the jumping height, the size of the balloon, and the size of the crowds. For an AX7 balloon running with a jump height of 150 feet with a crowd of 50 people, 15 acres of land is sufficient. A change in the jumping height to three hundred feet may increase the land requirement to twenty five acres.

The jump zone should be corded off so the crowd will know to stay out of that area. This will keep the jumper's shoe from falling off the jumper and hitting an on-looking on the head.

Some commercial site owners try to find a piece of land that is close to heavy vehicle traffic for better publicity. Other site owners prefer the privacy of a secluded site. The arguments for either preference are the same as for a bridge site. Drivers who view someone jumping from a balloon tend to cause accidents. However, that is one way to get free publicity.

While bungeeing over water may save a life or limb of a jumper, it is a challenge to land a balloon that is tethered over water. Whenever the balloon is landed, the jumper and the balloon get wet. It is difficult to launch a tethered balloon from dry land and make the balloon move over water for the jump because balloons do whatever the wind asks of them. If the wind directed the balloon over the water, the same wind will not push it back to dry land.

The average time required for a 150 foot jump is about 3 to 5 minutes, with good weather and a well-trained crew. The time required per jump from a balloon will run higher than a bridge or crane jump. This is because balloons have a mind of their own, and the balloon responds to changes in wind direction and strength, and temperature changes. A balloon may just decide to stay up in the air a few seconds longer, and there is not much the pilot can do to make the balloon cool faster. A wind blast may cause the balloon to drop altitude enough that the jump master decides to hold the jumper back until the altitude is increased to a clearly sufficient height.

If there ever was a platform that is not recommended for special jumps such as the water dunk, soda can grab, or negative jump, the hot air balloon is that platform. It is the most unstable platform used in commercial jumping. It can easily drop ten feet in one second. If the jumper has a fifty foot clearance, that ten foot drop causes no worry. However, if the jumper is performing the soda grab and is coming within four feet of the ground, that ten foot drop is serious.

The most common commercial jump heights from the balloon are 150 feet and 300 feet. It is important that the balloon is at the intended altitude before the jumper leaps. Most pilots depend upon an altimeter to confirm their altitude. One small problem with that method is that since the altimeter uses the air pressure to determine the altitude, and since the air pressure can change considerably within a half-hour period, the altimeter can be wrong by fifteen feet after a three hour jump session. It is suggested that a the air pressure be checked regularly via the local weather service. Another suggestion is to have a second, even third, method of determining the balloon's altitude, maybe a landmark that is visible to the pilot at a particular height. If it can be kept out of the path of the jumper, a measured cord attached at the equator of the envelope with a weight and flag on the end could be a visual check. If the flag is touching the ground, the balloon is too low for the jump.

For a jump from a crane or bridge, the jumper should come no closer to the ground than the distance equal to one-fourth of the jump height. Because the balloon is less stable than a crane or bridge, that safety margin should be increased. A person jumping from a hot air balloon should come no closer to the ground than the distance equal to one-third the jump height. If the balloon's height is 150 feet, the jumper should come no closer to the ground than 50 feet.

When the jumper is ready to be attached to the bungee cords, his harness(es) are clipped onto the cords, and the jumper climbs into the balloon, which is resting on the ground. Then the pilot takes the balloon to the desired height and the jumper climbs out of the basket, either onto the side of the basket or onto a jumping shelf. The countdown is given, and the jumper leaps into the air. After he has quit bouncing and rebounding, the balloon is lowered until the jumper has his feet on the ground. The ground crew takes the harnesses off of the cords, and the jumper walks away. The balloon hesitates for a few seconds after the jumper's weight is unloaded, then settles the rest of the way to the ground for the next jumper.

It is difficult for a jumper to do a clean jump if he is required to jump from a sitting position from the side of the basket. If he is provided with a jumping shelf, he can fall backward, dive, or whatever he desires. The shelf does not have to be any bigger than twelve to eighteen inches wide and nine to twelve inches deep, basically large enough to place his feet on. (Figure 4-3) Some jumping shelves are bolted onto the side or bottom of the basket while other are simply hung over the edge of the basket. This is another challenge for the project engineer.

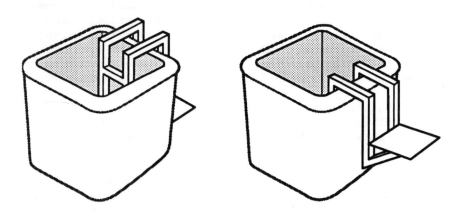

Figure 4-3 Balloon Jumping Shelf

Chapter Summary:

Legalities:

- In October of 1990, a memorandum was issued by the FAA that instructed that any type of airworthiness or operational approval should not be issued for any balloon modified to incorporate bungee jumping operations.
- A second FAA memo was published in May of 1991 giving guidance to field inspectors to handle the requests for approval of modifications to the balloons for bungee jumping as they would for modifications for any other purpose.
- If the modifications are more complex, the balloonist may have to apply for either an engineering letter of approval, or a Supplemental Type Certificate (STC).
- Some balloon bungee sites got around all the above process by decertifying their balloon.

Selecting a Hot Air Balloon:

- The balloon sizes that are most popular for bungee jumping are AX7, AX8, and AX9.
- It is best to attach the load of the jumper to the envelope cables.
- The price of a balloon can run between ten and fifty thousand dollars.

Operational Issues:

- Balloons can only be flown during sunrise and sunset, and times of little or no wind and no rain or snow.
- The plot of land for the site should be around fifteen to twenty five acres.
- The spectator area should be roped off.
- A site located near a high-traffic area can be good and bad.
- It is difficult to tether a balloon over water.
- The average time required for a 150 foot jump is about 3 to 5 minutes. A balloon is the most unstable platform used in commercial jumping, and is not recommended for special jumps.
- The most common commercial jump heights from the balloon are 150 feet and 300 feet.
- It is important that the balloon is at the intended altitude before the jumper leaps.
- A person jumping from a hot air balloon should come no closer to the ground than the distance equal to one-third the jump height.
- After he has quit bouncing and rebounding, the balloon is lowered until the jumper has his feet on the ground.
- A jumping shelf allows for cleaner style from the jumper.

CHAPTER FIVE

Using a Crane as a Jumping Platform

Cranes have become the commercial bungee platform of choice. They can be used in hot weather, in cold weather, during the day, at night, even when a breeze is present. The following are some of the concerns a site owner deals with when using a crane as a bungee platform.

LEGALITIES

A potential crane bungee site owner has to decide whether to buy or lease a crane. It is next to impossible to find a crane owner who is willing to lease his crane for bungee jumping. The crane owner accepts great financial risk from potential liability when he leases his crane for any purpose. When his crane is used for bungeeing, his liability risk is greater than when it is used for construction. Most crane owners are not anxious to take on the extra risk because the income from the bungee lease is a tiny percent of his overall income and is not worth the extra risk of loosing his entire business in a lawsuit.

The crane owner may demand that the lessee provide liability coverage for several million dollars. Most bungee insurance policies only provide coverage up to a million dollars. So, the lessee has to either find a insurance policy that provides the multi-million dollar coverage or find a crane owner who is willing to settle for a million dollar policy.

The potential crane bungee site owner's other option is to buy the crane. To purchase the crane, the bungeeist has to raise large amounts of capital. Then he has to figure out a way to make a profit sufficient enough to recover his capital. That sounds like it would not be very difficult for a business that brings in as much money as does bungee jumping. However, the site's expenses include payment for the crane, salaries for site crew, insurance, and bungee equipment. The payments for the crane can be as much as $9,000 a month for rental. To purchase a used crane, a person can expect to pay anywhere from $70,000 to $150,000. A crew of at least five or six workers is needed. Insurance can cost fifteen percent of the site's gross income. Bungee equipment can cost about $3,000 initially, and wear and tear on the equipment can cost one to two dollars a jump. To cover the expenses and still make a profit requires a steady flow of customers and some excellent business management.

Each city or county has regulations concerning the placement and use of a construction crane for commercial purposes. Some areas require that the land the crane is on is large enough that should the crane fall over, it would not fall onto property other than the site's land.

Access roads, sufficient area for parking, paved parking, landscaping, available fire hydrants, amusement permits, site owner background checks, workman's compensation, taxes, public rest rooms, fencing, water drainage, ground lighting and office buildings can be issues that a commercial site owner has to consider. The site may have to be inspected prior to opening for business by a government inspector. The site-owner-to-be should contact city hall for regulation and permit information.

Another government agency that impacts the preparation of a commercial bungee site is the Occupational Health and Safety Administration (OSHA). Their purpose is to ensure that the employees of any business have a safe and healthy environment in which to work. An example of how a commercial crane bungee site is affected by OSHA is that there are very strict and limiting requirements for workers who are in the suspended cage.

OSHA also certifies the cage that is used as a jumping shelf (figure 5-1). The standards that are used for the jumping cage are the same that are used for a cage used for construction purposes. The floors and the sides have to be solid and made of specific materials. The sides have to be a certain height. There has to be a locking safety gate at the entrance to the cage. Primarily, OSHA looks to see that the cage has been engineered by a certified engineer and assembled by a certified welder.

SELECTING A CRANE

There are basically three types of construction cranes. One is the tower crane. (Figure 5-2) These cranes are permanent, and are the cranes most commonly used for extreme heights. When tower cranes are assembled, a concrete foundation is laid, and the vertical main boom is built to the required height, which can be up to 280 feet high. Then the horizontal boom is added. When the crane is built, it looks like a "T". The horizontal boom can rotate 360 degrees on a horizontal plane, but is not capable of rotating on a vertical plane. Tower cranes are used for building skyscrapers because they are very stable, and

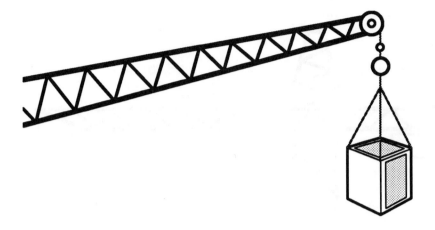

Figure 5-1 Cage used as a jumping shelf.

can pick up supplies from the ground and lower them to any part of the building.

A second type of crane is the conventional crane. (Figure 5-3) The base of the crane is on wheels, and is driven onto the site where it is to be set up. The rest of the crane is brought in on other trucks. The boom is built from forty foot sections of solid lattice "building blocks". It is built to the required height. Then the jib is attached. Both the boom and the jib can move in almost any direction, much like the human arm. The base of the crane is like a person's shoulder, the boom is like the upper arm, and the jib is like the lower arm. The jib is called an offset jib because it is capable of moving.

The third type of crane is the hydraulic crane. (Figure 5-4) The boom is telescopic. It is extended and retracted during use. The crane is usually not disassembled for relocation. Rather, it is totally retracted into itself and lays down on the base. Then the crane is a self-contained vehicle that can be driven to the next site.

The mobile cranes, which are the hydraulic and conventional cranes, are the styles normally used in bungee jumping. The permanent tower crane is usually not used since it is expensive to set it up at a bungee site that may be moved to a new location after a few months. Also, it is difficult to bring in enough revenue to cover the expense of purchasing or leasing a crane that size. However, the disadvantage of a mobile crane is that they are unstable at extreme height. They usually are limited to 150 to 200 feet for bungee jumping.

A used mobile crane can be purchased for somewhere between $70,000 and $150,000. A crane can be leased for about $9,000 a month. The crane owner will charge a delivery and pick-up fee, usually around $4,000 to $5,000 for each delivery or pick-up.

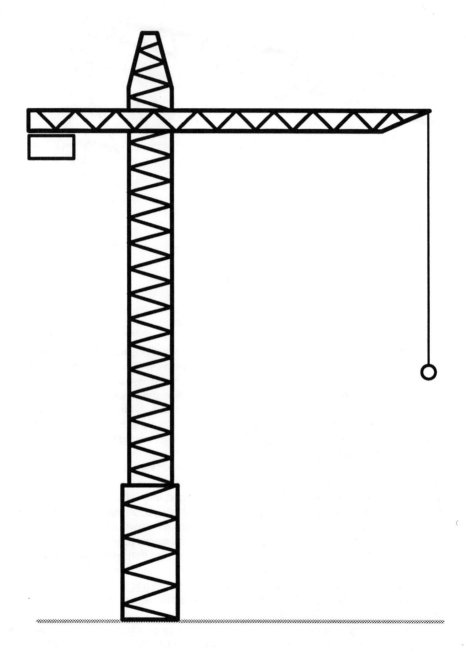

Figure 5-2 Tower Crane

BUNGEE JUMPING

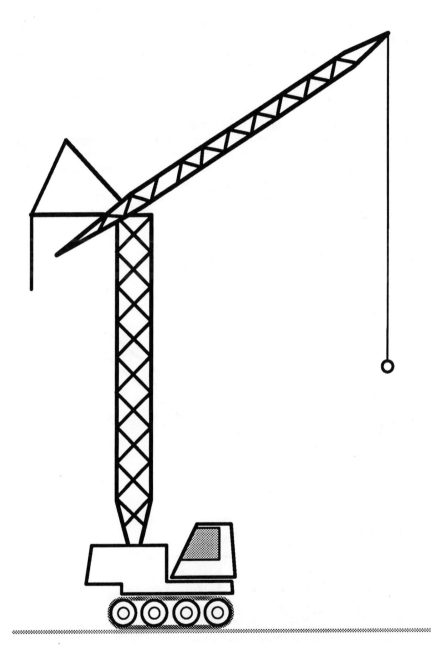

Figure 5-3 Conventional Crane

If the crane is an older one, it may not have a safety feature called an anti-two block brake system. (Figure 5-5) It is a newer feature that is required by OSHA and most insurance companies. The load bearing cables are usually attached at the end of the jib, and a headache ball is attached to the cables. Below the headache ball, the jumping cage is suspended. The anti-two block brake system is attached to the cables a few feet above the headache ball. It is a second smaller ball with a brake switch. When the cables are retracted and the smaller ball comes in contact with the jib, the brake switch is activated and the cable cannot be retracted any further.

If the anti-two block brake is not on the crane, it is possible that the cable can be retracted too far, and the headache ball be pulled tight against the jib. That causes the cable to be jammed and the cage can't be lowered back to the ground. That happens because the cable is pulled so taut that the mechanism that reverses the direction of the cable can't be released.

It is also possible for the cable to continue pulling after the headache ball contacts the jib. If that happens, the jib is forced upward. That would be a pretty wild ride for the jumper attached to the cage.

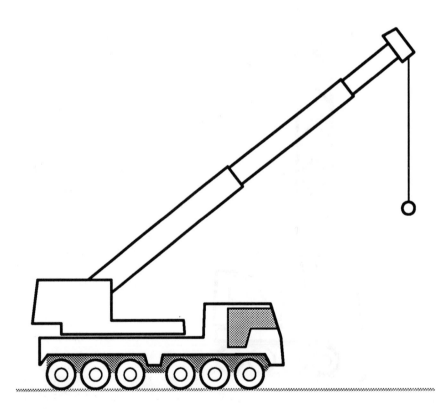

Figure 5-4 Hydraulic Crane

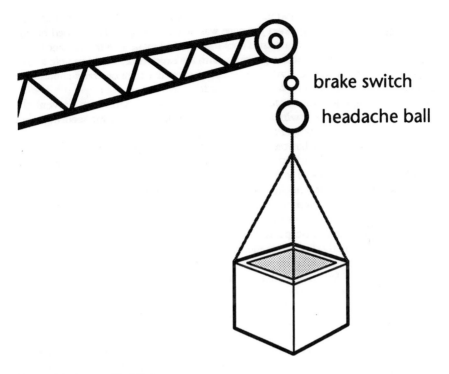

brake switch

headache ball

Figure 5-5 Anti-two Block Brake

The installation of an anti-two block brake system on a crane can run as much as $8,000 to $12,000.

OPERATIONAL ISSUES

An advantage of a crane over a hot air balloon as a bungee platform is that the time required per jump is less for a crane than for a balloon. A smooth running crane site can average three to four minutes per jump. The crane is not subject to the whims of the wind, and can move up and down faster than a balloon.

A common height for a crane bungee jump is about 150 to 200 feet. That height is high enough to please the extra brave jumpers and reasonable enough to appeal to the less brave. The maximum height of the jump will be determined by the type of crane used and its stability at extreme height. Guidelines for the crane's stability is available from the manufacturer of the crane.

The jumper should come no closer to the ground than the distance equal to one fourth the height of the jumping cage. If the cage is raised to two hundred feet for the jump, the jumper should come no closer than fifty feet from the ground.

It is strongly recommended that a jump master is in the cage with the jumper. There are several reasons for this recommendation. An average first-time jumper will be in dire need of constant encouragement and moral support. The jump master provides that second-by-second support as well as step-by-step direction on what the jumper is suppose to do, and when to do it. It is not good news if a jumper was to get scared and decide to jump when the cage was only half-way to its intended height. The jump master, with his calm and cool head, would make sure the jumper leaped at the proper time. Also, the jump master, with his experience, would be able to spot potential trouble with the cords, harnesses, or even the cage or crane cables. It is difficult to see some problems from the ground.

The jumping platform should be secured in some manner to prevent the cage from spinning and swinging. If cables or ropes are used for securing, they need to be clear of the jumper's potential jump and rebound path.

When the jumper has completed his jump and is swinging back and forth on the end of the bungee cords, the cage and jumper are lowered. The jumper touches the ground and is unhooked as the cage comes the rest of the way down to the ground. Then the next customer is hooked onto the cords and is loaded into the cage.

There are many methods of attaching the cage to the crane. If a cage is used that is normally used for construction purposes, the cage will already be ready to attach to the crane. The person who engineers the cage design would also mastermind the method of attachment.

One way of attaching the bungee cords to the crane is with two 5/8 inch or 3/4 inch steel braided chokers that are about ten to twelve feet long and are rated for at least ten thousand pounds. The chokers are attached to the headache ball and ran through the cage, through a hole in the middle of the cage floor, and hung a few feet below the cage. One choker is about six inches longer than the other and is the load bearing choker. (Figure 5-6) The other choker acts as a back-up. Should the load bearing choker fail, the second one would catch the load. The reason the load is not supported by both chokers simultaneously is because if there were a failure, both chokers would fail simultaneously and there would be no back-up.

An issue to consider when engineering a bungee jumping system from a crane is the ability of the pulley system to stand up to the repetitive jolts resulting from bungee jumping. The pulley system includes wheels, steel cables, motors, and brake systems that were designed to handle heavy loads that produced a steady pressure. They were not designed to withstand sudden shocks. The manufacturers of each system component can provide information on the effects of the jolting.

There needs to be a side-to-side clearance sufficient for the movements of the jumper. The side-to-side clearance should be equal to 150% of relaxed cord length or 75% of extended cord length.[3] If the cage is 200 feet high and the jumper wishes to fall 150 feet, the relaxed cord should equal 75 feet and expand to 150 feet. The side-to-side clearance should be at least 113 feet in any direction.

It is common for a commercial site to offer water dunking from a crane. While it is smarter to do this type of jump from a crane rather than a hot air balloon since the crane is more stable, the author does not recommend doing so in a commercial setting. It is too easy to make a mistake on the height of the cage, or miscalculate the expansion of the cord based on the weight of the jumper when working with many jumpers in a time-sensitive atmosphere.

A negative jump is sometimes offered at a commercial crane site. This is where a jumper is attached to bungee cords that are in turn attached to a crane. The jumper is held on the ground by a group of people or by some other type of

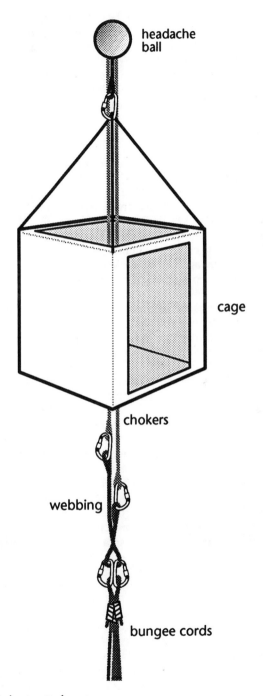

Figure 5-6 Chokers for bungee attachment.

anchor, such as a car. The crane pulls the cage upwards and creates tension in the cords. Then the group of people let go of the jumper and the jumper flies towards the cage. (See Figure 1-5) The author feels that this is a jump that should be left to the professional stuntmen who get paid to put their life in jeopardy. It is very difficult to predict the direction or distance that the jumper will travel. He could easily hit the cage or some other part of the crane either on the way up, or on the way down if he shoots higher than the cage.

Chapter Summary:

Legalities:

- It is next to impossible to find a crane owner who is willing to lease his crane for bungee jumping.
- The payments for the crane can be as much as $9,000 a month for rental. To purchase a used crane, a person can expect to pay anywhere from $70,000 to $150,000.
- Each city or county has regulations concerning the placement and use of a construction crane for commercial purposes.
- A government agency that impacts the preparation of a commercial bungee site is the Occupational Health and Safety Administration (OSHA).

Selecting a Crane:

- There are basically three types of construction cranes, tower, conventional and hydraulic.
- Older cranes may not have a safety feature called an anti-two block brake system, which OSHA requires.

Operational Issues:

- A smooth running crane site can average three to four minutes per jump.
- A common height for a crane bungee jump is about 150 to 200 feet.
- The jumper should come no closer to the ground than the distance equal to one fourth the height of the jumping cage.
- It is strongly recommended that a jump master is in the cage with the jumper.
- One way of attaching the bungee cords to the crane is with two 5/8 inch or 3/4 inch steel braided chokers.
- The pulley system may not be able to stand up to the repetitive jolts resulting from bungee jumping.
- The side-to-side clearance should be equal to 150% of relaxed cord length or 75% of extended cord length.
- A common special jump offered at crane sites is a negative jump, which is a very high risk jump.

CHAPTER SIX

Using a Tower as a Jumping Platform

The description of a tower that is used as a bungee jumping platform is a fairly inclusive one. Basically, a tower is any bungee platform that is not a hot air balloon, crane, or bridge. It usually is a stationary structure. Some towers have been built for the purpose of bungee jumping, others were adapted to that purpose. It is difficult to discuss towers as platforms in great detail because of the variety of styles. However, there are a few issues that should be considered.

LEGALITIES

The owner of the tower would inquire about the building codes that apply to the tower at the local government offices. The tower may fall under the codes of a bridge or a building. The design would have to be approved by a certified engineer. If the tower is already build, it would have to meet certain structural codes and may have to be improved to meet those codes.

The zoning regulations that apply to a tower would be similar to those that apply to a crane site. Refer to the previous chapter for that information.

A tower site is subject to local commercial regulations and permits. Information on those requirements would be found at city hall.

The Occupational Safety and Health Administration (OSHA) is involved in the startup of a tower site. They review the engineering of the jumping shelf and the retrieval system, and stipulate who is authorized to ride on the jumping shelf with the jumper. Again, refer to the previous chapter for more information on the involvement of OSHA. The crane site and tower site are affected by many of the same legal issues.

SELECTING A TOWER

A person looking into a tower bungee site has to decide whether to design and build a tower from scratch, or to adapt an already existing tower. The advantage of designing a tower specifically for bungeeing is that it can be designed for the most efficient service to the jumpers. It can be designed to take up a minimal amount of land. It can be built to the most desirable height. However, there is a large investment in the engineering and design. It costs big bucks to hire experts to design a tower. Also, when the design is being used for the first time, it has not been tested elsewhere. That means that the bugs haven't been worked out prior to the building of the tower. Those bugs can cause serious, costly and life-threatening problems.

A tower that is already built and that is adapted for bungee jumping purposes presents a few problems also. The structure can be bulkier than necessary, which wastes land and maintenance efforts. The bungee operation may not be as efficient as desired because of compromises due to unchangeable features of the tower. However, the tower is already designed and built, and the only engineering and building expenses pertain to changes that have to be made. Making changes take less time and money than does building from the ground up.

The ideal height for a tower can be anywhere from fifty feet to three hundred feet. Again, the most common heights for commercial sites are about 150 feet to 250 feet. The tower could be designed to offer a couple of different height options to its customers.

The tower could be built over water. The water may soften a fall if the bungee system failed and a jumper hit the ground. The site could offer a water dunk jump to the customer. However, the author feels that water dunks should not be done at a commercial site due to the chance of miscalculation. Each jumper has a different weight and jumping style that can change the fall distance by several feet. When the customer is suppose to dunk into the water, a miscalculation of a few feet could make him hit the bottom of the body of water.

One way to avoid the expense of designing a tower from scratch is to buy into a franchise. There is at least one franchise in the United States that offers the tower, bungee system, financing, and assistance with plowing through the legalities of setting up the site. The tower's design has been tested and tried, and also has been designed specifically for bungee jumping.

A person looking into setting up a tower for bungee jumping on his own can expect to pay somewhere between $10,000 and $50,000 for the engineering efforts, and at least another $50,000 to $400,000 to build the tower. Then he can plan on spending at least $30,000 for permits, inspections, legal fees, and other expenses to comply with local regulations.

The time required for designing and setting up a bungee tower site is much greater than it would be for a hot air balloon or crane. It can easily take six months to a year for an engineer to design the tower. Then the tower's owner has to get the plans approved and work through the local regulations and zoning laws. That can take several more months. The building of the tower is probably the easiest part of the whole effort. Depending upon the complexity of the tower, the weather, and the availability of the builders, it can take one to six months to build the tower and prepare the site for business.

If the tower is built near a high traffic area, there will be instant and free advertising as the car passengers see the bungee jumping happening. It would be very simple to draw a crowd. However, accidents happen when car drivers see a person jumping from a tower. If the police decide that the bungee jumping is a traffic hazard, they can take steps to get the site shut down. If the site owner has put money and time into setting up the site, he will be heartbroken if he has to shut it down. A tower doesn't move to the next town easily.

OPERATIONAL ISSUES

The time required per commercial jump should be less than the time required with any other platform. A tower is not subject to wind, it is stable, and it is designed specifically for bungee jumping. If the time required is not less than it is for a crane, it would be very close. A tower should be able to service a customer every three to four minutes.

A well-designed tower with multiple jump platforms should be able to average the launching of a jumper every thirty seconds.

The tower needs to be designed so that the jumper has sufficient clearance for side-to-side movement. The formula for figuring the minimum clearance is the same as it is for a crane. The side-to-side clearance should be equal to 150% of relaxed cord length or 75% of extended cord length.3 If the jumping shelf is 200 feet high and the jumper wishes to fall 150 feet, the relaxed cord should equal 75 feet and expand to 150 feet. The side-to-side clearance should be at least 113 feet in any direction.

The land area requirement for a tower will usually be less than it will be for a crane. That is because with a crane, there has to be enough distance from the location of the crane to the edge of the bungee site property to allow room for the crane to fall over should that happen. The tower site usually doesn't have to have that allowance because the chance of the the tower falling over is very slight. The site owner still has to consider parking space and a large jump zone. The site should have at least five acres for parking in addition to the acreage needed for the jump zone and tower.

The design of the jumping shelf or cage would depend upon the tower design and retrieval system design. The shelf could be stationary, similar to the jumping shelf for a bridge. The jumper would get to the shelf by stairs or separate elevator and would be lowered by a pulley system. On the other hand, the jumping shelf could be mobile, much like the jumping cage on a crane. Then the cage would be lowered to the jumper on the ground, he would ride up in the cage, jump from the cage, and the cage would lower with the jumper when he was finished jumping.

There are guidelines set up by OSHA that pertain to the jumping shelf, and those guidelines are discussed in the previous chapter. The tower site is under the jurisdiction of OSHA and is subject to their regulations.

The methods of attaching the bungee equipment to the tower can be as varied as the design of the tower. Guidance can be drawn from the crane and bridge guidelines as well as the bungee system manufacturer.

Chapter Summary:

Legalities:
- The owner of the tower would inquire about the building codes that apply to the tower at the local government offices.

Selecting a Tower:
- A person looking into a tower bungee site has to decide whether to design and build a tower from scratch, or to adapt an already existing tower.
- The ideal height for a tower can be anywhere from fifty feet to three hundred feet.
- The tower could be built over water.
- A person building a tower can expect to spend a minimum of one hundred thousand dollars.
- There can be problems with using a tower near a high-traffic area.

Operational Issues:
- A tower should be able to service a customer every three to four minutes.
- The side-to-side clearance should be equal to 150% of relaxed cord length or 75% of extended cord length.
- The land area requirement for a tower will usually be less than it will be for a crane.
- The design of the jumping shelf or cage would depend upon the tower design and retrieval system design.
- The tower site is under the jurisdiction of OSHA and is subject to their regulations.

Bungee Cords

The component of the bungee jumping system that gives the sport its name is the bungee cord. The bungee cord is the elastic rope that is attached to the jumping platform on one end and to the jumper on the other end. The bungee cords that are produced for the military are used by some branches of the military to reduce the opening shock of a parachute when dropping tanks and other heavy equipment from aircrafts.

There are many kinds of bungee cord. An entire book could be written just on the specifications of every bungee cord. However, for the purpose of conserving space, all information in this chapter, unless otherwise noted, refers to the bungee cord known as MIL-SPEC. MIL-SPEC bungee cords are cords that are constructed to military specifications. There are three types of MIL-SPEC cords, and many widths in each type. The MIL-SPEC cord referred to within this chapter is the 5/8 inch Type I cord. To obtain a copy of the current military specification document, request document MIL-C-5651 from: Systems Engineering and Standardization Department (Code 93), Naval Air Engineering Center, Lakehurst, NJ 08733.[5]

CONSTRUCTION

Bungee cord is made of rubber on the inside, and cotton braid on the outside. The rubber strands are made from natural or synthetic rubber, or a mixture thereof. The yarns for the exterior braid are made from cotton. The exterior cover may have one or two layers of braid, known as single or double braided sheathing.

The bungee cords used for bungee jumping have a double braided sheathing. The military specifications require that the bungee cords have two layers of cotton sheathing. Some cord that is manufactured for consumers other than the military use a layer of cotton and a layer of nylon sheathing, or one or two layers of nylon with no cotton. Usually cord that has nylon sheathing has a higher breaking strength than cords with only cotton sheathing. However, it is important to understand that even if the nylon covered cords meet and exceed the military standards in every other aspect, they are not MIL-SPEC cords. If a site owner were taken to court due to a bungee cord failure, he would have documentation for MIL-SPEC cords, but may not have documentation for a nylon sheathed cord unless the manufacturer of the cord had legitimate documentation.

MIL-SPEC bungee cord is available in diameter of 1/8 inch to 13/16 inch.[6] The diameter most commonly used in bungee jumping is the 5/8 inch cord. Cord other than MIL-SPEC can be as thick as 1 inch. It is not necessarily true that a 1 inch cord is stronger than a 5/8 inch cord because the breaking strength can vary based upon the number of layers of sheathing, the strength of the sheathing, the material used in making the sheathing, the type of rubber used, and the method of cord construction. The main factor to be concerned about is the breaking strength, also known as tensile strength. This is the maximum strength that a cord can be subjected to without failure. The 5/8 inch MIL-SPEC is required to have a minimum tensile strength of five hundred pounds.[7] Most 5/8 inch bungee cord are manufactured to have a breaking strength of more than 1000 pounds.

Bungee cord performance can be compromised due to age. The military specifications require that the cord should be shipped to the consumer no later than six months after it is manufactured. To enforce that requirement, the main color of the outer sheathing of the cord shows the date the cord was manufactured. The colors are as follows: black (1990), green (1991), red (1992), blue (1993), yellow (1994). For succeeding years, this cycle is repeated.

In addition to the year, the outer sheathing indicates the quarter year of manufacture by the minority color. The colors are as follows: red (January—March), blue (April—June), green (July—September), yellow (October—December).[8]

PERFORMANCE

A cord elongates when a load is placed on the cord. With no load, the cord is at zero percent elongation. When a 100 foot length of 5/8 inch cord is stressed with a 140 pound load, the cord has experienced a fifty percent elongation. That means the cord has increased from 100 feet to 150 feet. With a 205 pound load, the cord is at seventy five percent elongation, from 100 feet to 175 feet. A 300 pound load produces a one hundred percent elongation, which stretches the cord to 200 hundred feet. The highest percent of elongation that a 5/8 inch cord will tolerate, known as the ultimate elongation, is 140 percent. A MIL-SPEC cord is required to have a tensile strength of at least five hundred pounds. However, in most cases, the actual strength is 1,300 pounds, the load that will produce a 140 percent elongation.[9] (Figure 7-1).

A. Relaxed Cord

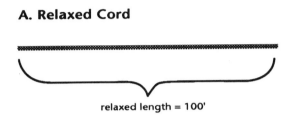

relaxed length = 100'

B. Cord with 140 pound load

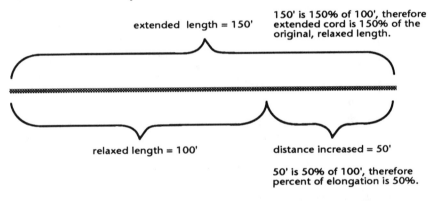

extended length = 150'

150' is 150% of 100', therefore extended cord is 150% of the original, relaxed length.

relaxed length = 100'

distance increased = 50'

50' is 50% of 100', therefore percent of elongation is 50%.

Figure 7-1 Relation of percent of elongation to extended and relaxed length.

If those ratios were plotted on a graph, they would produce a parabola (Figure 7-2). That means the greatest elongation occurs with the initial application of the load. As the load increases, the rate of elongation decreases. That is why the jumper is gradually slowed to a stop. The cord stretches easily when the jumper is falling at a fast rate and first begins putting stress on the cords. As the stress from the jumper's weight increases, the cord stretches less and reduces the jumper's speed.

Even though the cord can expand to 240 percent of its relaxed length, it is recommended that the cord only extend to 200 percent of its relaxed length, which is to 100 percent elongation. There are a few reasons for this. It is a good

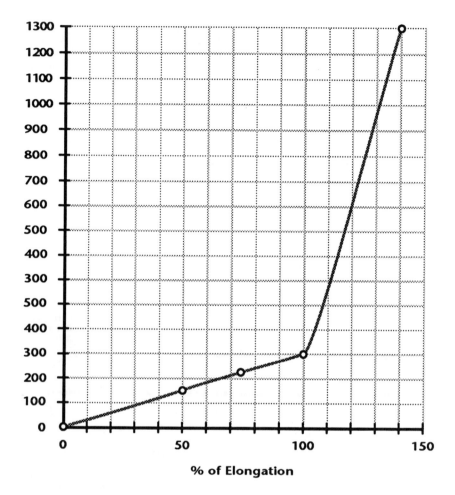

Figure 7-2 Elasticity Parabola

idea to leave a substantial safety margin. It is not a good idea to push the cord close to the ultimate elongation since that is the point of failure. One hundred percent is a good and safe elongation.

Another reason pertains to a flex cycle. "Flex cycle" is an expression meaning a cord has been stretched and relaxed one time. In the case of bungee jumping, a cycle is equal to a fall and rebound of a jumper. Therefore, a jumper may subject a cord to two or three cycles per jump. It is recommended that a cord be expanded to a one hundred percent elongation for maximum life of the cord during each cycle. If a cord consistently stretches more than that percent during its life, the cycle rating reduces. The MIL-SPEC cord rates at 50,000 cycles.

A comfortable and reasonable safety margin is to retire the cords after a number of jumps that is equal to one percent of the rated cycles. If a cord rates

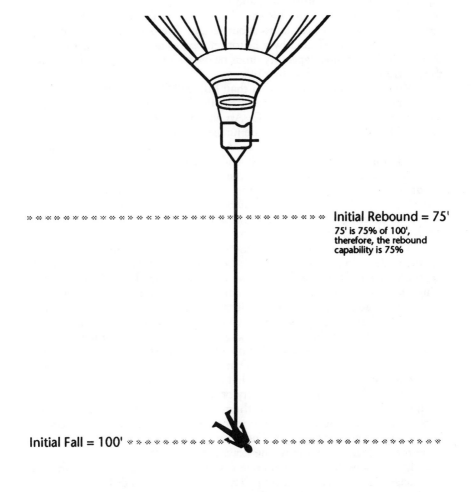

Initial Rebound = 75'
75' is 75% of 100',
therefore, the rebound
capability is 75%

Initial Fall = 100'

Figure 7-3 Rebound Capability

for 50,000 cycles, the cord should be retired after five hundred jumps. If a bungeeist wants to be on the safe side, a cord could be retired after two hundred jumps.

One guideline for knowing when a cord is reaching the end of its life considers the rebound capability of the cord. If on new cords, a jumper falls one hundred feet during his initial fall, and the cord elongates one hundred percent during that same initial fall, his initial rebound should be about seventy five feet. (Figure 7-3) That is equal to about seventy five percent of the initial fall. As a cord ages, it is effected by a factor referred to as drift. Drift is the loss of tension. If the rebound capability drops below about sixty percent due to drift, the cords are near the end of their life.

Keep in mind that cords other than MIL-SPEC may be capable of up to a ninety percent rebound, and their "red flag" rebound capability would be different than it is with MIL-SPEC. An advantage of using cords that have a greater rebound capability is that the jumper will experience a softer stop, and the rebound will feel more intense. Also, more bounces per jump can be expected from cords with a better rebound capability.

A third reason for not allowing the cord to be stretched to more than one hundred percent elongation is that the outer covering is designed to stay tight enough to keep dirt away from the rubber up to that elongation.[10] After that point, the covering may allow gaps that would permit dirt into the rubber. The dirt is capable of damaging the rubber.

The air temperature affects the elasticity of the bungee cord. If the temperature is low, the rubber will be less responsive. The jumpers will experience a harder stop, and less elongation and rebound. On the other hand, a high temperature will make the rubber softer. The jumper will experience a gentler ride, and he will fall a greater distance and will have a better rebound.

In the desert, the temperature changes greatly, and quickly, when the sun rises or sets. In other climates, the change is less dramatic but still exists. That means the distance a jumper will fall on a particular set of cords can change by as much as five feet within an hour. That is a scary thought when a commercial site is offering water dunks in a pond that is only ten feet deep.

Extreme heat, sunlight, humidity or moisture can affect the performance of the cords, or possibly damage them. Heat tends to age the cord. The ultraviolet sun rays breaks down the rubber. Moisture and humidity encourage the rubber and coverings to rot. These issues should be considered during the use of the cords as well as during the storage of the cords.

It is obvious that more than one cord should be used to support the load of a bungee jumper. The industry policy is to use three cords for jumpers who weigh between 80 and 150 pounds, four cords for up to two hundred pounds, and five cords for up to 250 pounds. It is usually not economical to set up a bungee system for jumpers over 250 pounds or under about 80 pounds because the demand is usually not worth the extra effort and expense. That is why many sites will enforce a weight limit. It is not because it can't be done or that the platform wouldn't support the weight.

If a jumper is attached to too many cords for his weight, he will experience a hard stop. His weight will not expand the cords to the length needed for a gentle ride and enjoyable rebound. A jumper who attaches to too few cords will receive a tremendously gentle ride, but the cords will be that much closer to failure since the safety factor is lessened.

FINISHING THE ENDS

The ends of the cords have to have some kind of loop or eye in order to attach to the neighboring bungee system components. It is a challenge to find a loop or eye that will hold up under the extreme demands placed upon the end.

There are no cut and dried rules for this challenge. Most site operators will not disclose their method for finishing the ends, and will cover their ends so that customers cannot see the method. The covering also acts to protect the jumper from coming in contact with the hardware. Some distributors of bungee systems provide the cords already finished or will provide direction on finishing the end.

It is the author's opinion that tying the ends in knots is one of the more dangerous methods for finishing the ends. If this method is used, it is with much trepidation.

The preferred method to finish an end is to attach software to the cord and have the software attach to the neighboring system component. The software can be a static cord or webbing. Static cord is a cylindrical rope with very low stretch, (Figure 7-4) and webbing is a non-elastic flat rope that looks like the handles on a gym bag (Figure 7-5). Both types of rope are designed to handle a load while bent into a knot. The static cord can be attached to the bungee cord with a self-tightening knot, such as a prusik loop (Figure 7-6). The cord remains straight because the prusik loop is engineered to grab onto a straight rope or cord. A safety knot may be tied into the end of the cord, but that knot would not carry any load.

The static cord can attach to the neighboring component, or it can be attached to webbing that would in turn attach to the neighboring component.

One other method to finish the end of a bungee cord is to bend the end of the cord over once and then fasten the loop with whipping. Whipping is the waxed string used to bind two cords together tightly. Usually whipping is applied when the cord stretches to about one hundred percent elongation. Then the cord relaxes. (Figure 7-7) This causes the whipping to be very tight and strong when the cord relaxes, and is able to hold when the cord stretches to a thinner diameter. Webbing or static cord can be bound in with the bungee cord for an alternate method of attaching software to the cord. One danger with whipping is that the whipping is so tight when the cord relaxes that it can cut into the cord covering and possibly into the rubber.

The hardware, such as a carabiner, can be hooked onto the cord end, or onto the static cord or webbing. The carabiner at one end of the cord hooks into the jumper's harness assembly. The carabiner at the other end hooks into the platform assembly.

A potential problem with the attachment of the carabiner to the bungee cord is that the carabiner can cut into the cord. The cord is expensive to replace or difficult to refinish if damaged by the carabiner. A better method is to attach software to the bungee cord, and the carabiner to the software. The

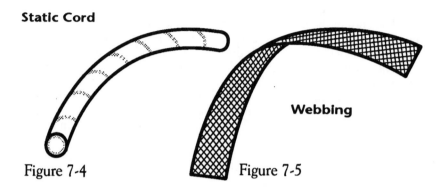

Static Cord

Webbing

Figure 7-4   Figure 7-5

Figures 7-4 & 7-5 Static cord and webbing.

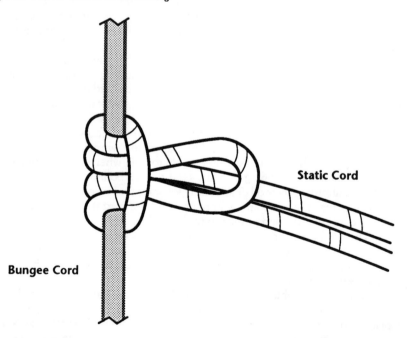

Static Cord

Bungee Cord

Figure 7-6 Prusik knot

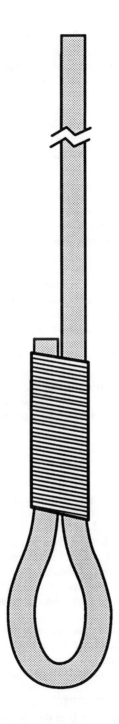

Figure 7-7 Bungee cord with whipping.

software can more easily be replaced, and in fact, usually can stand up to wear from the carabiner better than can the bungee cord.

The finished ends should be capable of handling at least five times the stress to which they will be subjected. Keep in mind that one cord is not going to handle all of the stress created by the jumper, it will be divided between all of the cords. The finished end will have to tolerate steady pull as well as sharp jolts. The bungee cord will become thinner as a load is applied. Just because the whipping or software or bungee cord rates to a particular tensile strength, that does not mean that the finished end will have the same tensile strength. The software and bungee cord are rated for use in a direct pull situation. The finished end is making abnormal use of the cords. The whipping will be affected differently. Stress will be carried by bent cords. Because of the abnormal use, the finished end should be tested to failure several times. The testing should be by the site owner if he is designing his own finished ends, or by the cord's manufacturer is the manufacturer is finishing the ends.

It is recommended that the manufacturer or distributor of the cord finishes the ends rather than the site owner. In most cases, the manufacturer has the resources to do extensive testing, and will have access to advanced technical data. Most site owners will only have access to a "back-yard" testing system of trees and car bumpers. In addition, the manufacturer will usually have access to the industrial equipment required to produce a strong, tight finished end.

Due to the recent growth of the industry, it should not be difficult to find a manufacturer who finishes the ends. However, just because the site owner does not have to finish his own ends, he should still know the engineering behind the finishing method. He should know the limitations of the finished end, how it is held together, and how extensively it has been tested and by whom.

SAFETY CONCERNS

The cord covering is usually stronger than the rubber, and serves as a sort of back-up to the rubber. Not only that, it seems to absorb the wave of shock. The cover also protects the rubber from dirt, sunlight, and moisture. However, it is difficult to prove that covered cord is better suited to bungee jumping than is uncovered cord because comparative data is not widely available.

It is common belief that a double covered cord is stronger and more durable than a single covered cord. A double cord may be covered in two layers of cotton, two layers of nylon, or a layer of each. The nylon covering is usually stronger than the cotton, and provides better protection for the rubber from moisture and dirt.

If a cord is not covered with two layers of cotton sheathing, it cannot be labeled as a MIL-SPEC cord. However, a cord with a different sheathing configuration can meet the performance requirements set forth by the MIL-SPEC documentation, and is as capable of performing the needed functions as a MIL-SPEC cord.

Common practice with MIL-SPEC cords is to increase the number of cords used by one per each fifty pounds of the jumper's weight. This means that there is between three and five cords being used at any particular time. The multiple cord system allows for each cord to be backed up by the other cords. If one cord breaks, the other cords still hold the load and only allow the load to drop a few feet further. (Figure 7-8)

A single cord system does not allow for that back-up. Most bungee systems outside of the United States and some within use the single cord system. The cord

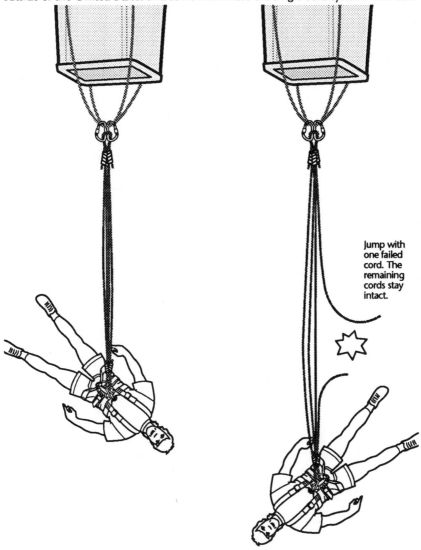

Jump with one failed cord. The remaining cords stay intact.

Figure 7-8 Multi-cord system provides its own back-up system.

is usually uncovered, and is about one inch in diameter. The breaking strength of the single cord is relatively close to the collective breaking strength of the MIL-SPEC multi-cord system. It is common belief within the United States that the multi-cord system with covered cords is better than the single cord system with uncovered cords that used outside of the United States.

One disadvantage of the multi-cord system is that when the cords relax during a rebound, each cord tends to go its separate direction. This can allow for one cord to go to one side of the jumper's head or other body part and another cord to go to the other side. When the cord expands again, the poor jumper will wish he were not in that position. To keep this from happening, velcro straps can be attached along the length of the set of cords. This allows the cords to act as one cord. A very strong velcro is required because the straps take a beating and don't stay on very well. Another thought is to run a nylon sock, something like panty hose, along the length of the cords.

The bungee cord needs to be cared for in a very special manner. It should be protected from moisture, heat, prolonged exposure to sunlight, dirt (especially sand) and elongation beyond the recommended percentage. When a cord is rebounding less than sixty percent of the distance of the initial fall, the cords should be retired. If the cord's cover is bunching, or the rubber has a "hernia" and is pushing through the cover (Figure 7-9), that is another sign the cord is damaged and the cord should be retired. The same is true if the cover or any part of the rubber has a cut or a worn spot. The entire length of each cord should be inspected before and after each day of use. It is easy to miss a small indication of trouble, and if the cord is inspected twice per day of use, the chances of seeing a trouble spot are high. Also, sometimes an indication of trouble may show up only a few jumps before the cord fails or is otherwise compromised.

The rubber of the cord ages, and will break easier when it ages. The military will not allow cord to be sold if it is older than six months. It is usually

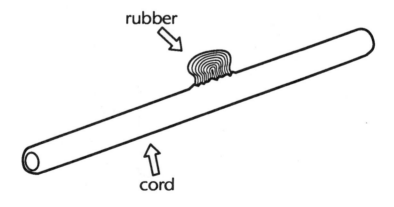

rubber

cord

Figure 7-9 "Hernia" on bungee cord.

recommended that the cord be destroyed when it is more than a year old, irregardless of how much it has been used.

One bungee system distributor demands that every cord be returned to him for inspection when it is to be retired. That is his way of making sure aged cord is not being used, and provides him with a way to look for problems with his cords.

Many sites cover the cord closest to the jumper with a padded covering, called a bumper (Figure 7-10). This protects the jumper from getting "bungee kisses" from the hardware or hard knots and stitching. The bumper can be anywhere from three feet to ten feet or more. The most common length is about five feet, about the length of a jumper. Also, the bumper gives the jumper something to hang onto if he gets scared.

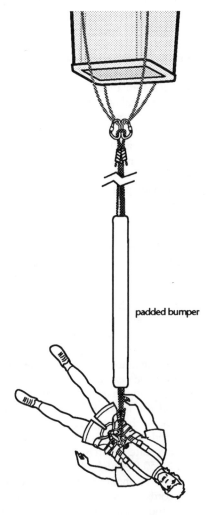

padded bumper

Figure 7-10 Bumper

SUPPLIERS

Through early 1991, it was very easy to obtain bungee cord because it was readily available through various distributors all over the country. Then the manufacturers of the cord became concerned about potential liability from the bungee jumping, and took steps to keep the cord away from bungeeists. The bungeeists were not prepared to manufacture their own, and so they obtained cord through various "under-the-table" means. About the time period of Fall 1991, bungee cord became more available because it was imported, and factories opened with the sole purpose of providing for the bungee industry. Now, the price of cord has become competitive because of the larger supply.

The best way to find a supplier of bungee cord is to contact the two most active bungee associations, the North American Bungee Association and the American Bungee Association. Unfortunately, due to the competitive nature of the industry, the contacts provided by either association are going to be exclusive. That is not necessarily bad because the associations will provide contacts that they believe are quality contacts. Those contacts will allow the bungeeist to get a foot into the network. The North American Bungee Association publishes a newsletter that will carry helpful information.

If a bungeeist prefers to find a distributor outside of the bungee network, he may contact large-scale cord manufacturers. Some mountain climbing shops or distributors of heavy military equipment may point him in the right direction. Keep in mind that most large-scale manufacturers either are unwilling to sell cord for the purpose of bungee jumping, or they have an exclusive agreement with a bungee distributor.

Bungee cord is rarely packaged at the manufacturer in lengths longer than one hundred feet unless it is specially prepared. That means that a distributor will normally offer it in lengths equal to or less than one hundred feet. Common lengths include twenty five, fifty, and one hundred. Lengths may be hooked together for longer lengths.

The price of the cord will vary depending on the quantity and lengths purchased, cord diameter, breaking strength, rebound capability, number of layers of covering, material type of covering, cycle rating and whether the ends are finished or raw. A person can expect to pay between three and fifteen dollars per foot for a MIL-SPEC 5/8 inch cord with finished ends. The MIL-SPEC cord will have a breaking strength of five hundred pounds. It's able to rebound to about seventy five percent of the initial fall with two layers of cotton covering, and it'll have a cycle rating of five hundred.

The bungeeist determines the amount of cord he needs by multiplying the height of the platform by seventy five percent (by sixty six percent if the platform is a hot air balloon) and then dividing that number by two. The first calculation results in the desired distance of the initial fall, also the length of the extended cord. The second calculation shows the length of the relaxed cord, which should be half of the extended cord length. (Figure 7-11) The bungeeist should order five cords of the calculated length to create a matched cord set.

If the jumping platform is 150 feet high, the desired fall distance is 113 feet, and the relaxed cord length would be about fifty five or sixty feet.

It is important that all cords in one set of cords be the same type of cord from the same manufacturer and manufactured at the same time. Each cord

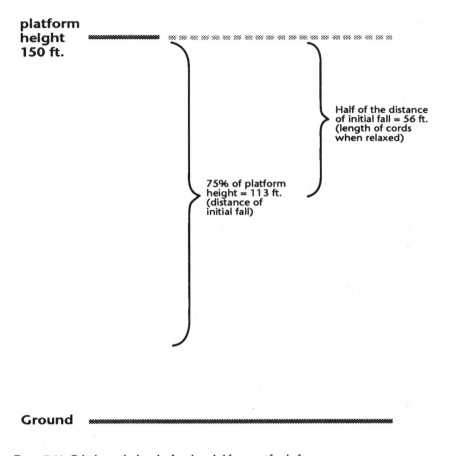

platform height 150 ft.

Half of the distance of initial fall = 56 ft. (length of cords when relaxed)

75% of platform height = 113 ft. (distance of initial fall)

Ground

Figure 7-11 Calculating the length of cord needed for a specific platform.

should have close to the same number of jumps as the rest of the cords in the set at any given moment. This ensures that each cord performs the same way as the rest of the cords in the set. It is also good business to have a spare set of cords available if that is feasible for the particular business.

When a bungeeist purchases a set of bungee cords, he should be given a set of design and performance specifications for that particular cord. If the distributor cannot provide the specifications and testing data, the bungeeist should be scared. That data shows that the cord has been tested and is not being produced in someone's basement with little concern for safety and professionalism. The distributor needs the data to protect his tail-end as much as the bungeeist needs the data to cover his tail-end. If the distributor doesn't have the data, that is an indication that he does not know the product he is selling.

If a lawsuit develops over an injury of death, that data will be needed to help prove the absence of negligence. It is a poor time to be looking for the data when the lawsuit is staring the bungeeist in the face. In fact, it is wise for the bungeeist to have his own copy of the specifications before he uses the cord. He has the right to insist that the specifications are provided. If a distributor is reluctant to provide that data before problems occur, he is not going to be any more cooperative in the face of a lawsuit. It is amazing how your best friend the distributor becomes very hard to find when the going gets tough. That is the way it is in the business world.

It is important to understand that if a cord is not manufactured to MIL-SPEC requirements, it is not a MIL-SPEC cord, even if the cord exceeds the requirements. MIL-SPEC requirements state that the cord will be covered with cotton. If a cord is covered with nylon, it is not MIL-SPEC, even though it meets and exceeds all the performance criteria. That is important to understand if a lawsuit develops in which the requirements are required to be brought into court. MIL-SPEC requirements are a proven and widely accepted standard, and will likely be looked upon favorably in court. Any other standards may be considered inferior unless they are backed by extensive documented testing done by certified engineers.

With the concern about MIL-SPEC requirements, lawsuits, and safety, the question is raised about the prudence of buying cord manufactured outside of the United States. It really doesn't matter where the cord is manufactured, it is important that it complies to the same criteria that is expected of the American-made cord. There has been superior cord produced outside of the United States that greatly exceeds the performance of the American cords and are backed by excellent testing.

Chapter Summary:
Construction:
- Bungee cord is made of rubber on the inside, and cotton braid on the outside.
- Usually cord that has nylon sheathing has a higher breaking strength than cords with only cotton sheathing.
- MIL-SPEC bungee cord is available in diameters of 1/8 inch to 13/16 inch.
- The 5/8 inch MIL-SPEC must have a tensile strength of at least five hundred pounds.
- Bungee cord performance can be compromised due to age.

Performance:
- The highest percent of elongation that a 5/8 inch cord will tolerate, known as the ultimate elongation, is 140 percent.
- It is recommended that the cord only be extended to one hundred percent elongation.
- The MIL-SPEC cord is rated at 50,000 cycles.
- If the rebound capability drops below about sixty percent due to drift, the cords are near the end of their life.
- The outer covering is designed to stay tight enough to keep dirt away from the rubber.
- The air temperature affects the elasticity of the bungee cord.
- Extreme heat, sunlight, humidity or moisture can affect the performance of the cords, or possibly damage them.
- Industry policy is to use three cords for jumpers who weigh less than 150

pounds, and an additional cord for each additional 50 pounds.

Finishing the Ends:
- One method is to tie the end of the cord into a knot.
- The preferred method to finish an end is to attach software to the cord and have the software attach to the neighboring system component.
- One other method is to bend the end of the cord over once and then fasten the loop with whipping.
- The finished ends should be capable of handling at least five times the stress to which they will subjected.
- It is recommended that the manufacturer or distributor of the cord finishes the ends rather than the site owner.

Safety Concerns:
- It is common belief that a double covered cord is stronger and more durable than a single covered cord.
- It is common belief within the United States that the multi-cord system with covered cords is better than the single cord system uncovered cords that is used outside of the United States.
- The bungee cord needs to be cared for in a very special manner.
- The entire length of each cord should be inspected before and after each day of use for signs of damage.
- Many sites cover the cord closest to the jumper with a padded bumper.

Suppliers:
- The best way to find a supplier of bungee cord is to contact the two most active bungee associations.
- Common lengths of cord include twenty five, fifty, and one hundred feet.
- A person can expect to pay between three and fifteen dollars per foot for a MIL-SPEC 5/8 inch cord with finished ends.
- When a bungeeist purchases a set of bungee cords, he should be given a set of design and performance specifications for that particular cord.
- It is important to understand that if a cord is not manufactured to MIL-SPEC requirements, it is not a MIL-SPEC cord, even if the cord exceeds the requirements.

CHAPTER EIGHT

Supplemental Bungee Equipment

W hile the bungee cords are a major part of a bungee operation, there are many other components. The components include the harnesses, carabiners, static lines, webbing, jumping shelf, safety equipment and air bags. The ways that each of these components is used varies at each site, but there are some performance and use guidelines that can be offered. It is very important that each component is checked, double checked, and triple checked each time there is a change to the equipment or when a harness is placed on a jumper. Each link of the bungee system should be checked every few jumpers.

There has been considerable concern about the ability of the equipment to stand up to repeated shocks. Each piece of equipment outside of the bungee cords was designed to withstand steady pressure and not repeated shock. There has been relatively little testing on the effects of the repeated shocks. It is worthy to note that if a climber experiences one single severe fall on his equipment, he retires all of his equipment. While it seems that the equipment is capable of handling many jumps, the industry members should be reminded that this equipment is delicate and should be handled with a wary eye because it can fail.

HARNESSES

Ankle

An ankle harness is a band or sheet of cloth that wraps around the ankle of a jumper. The harness is held in place by velcro, buckles, and/or straps and is used to attach a bungee jumper to bungee cords.

Jumpers who have jumped on ankle harnesses and full body harnesses have mixed opinions about which style provides the most intense adrenaline rush. Some jumpers believe that the full body harness makes them feel secure and cradled, maybe even restricted. The ankle harnesses let them forget they are attached and that allows for a more intense rush. Other jumpers say that the ankle harnesses are more awkward than they are worth and that the full body harness makes them feel like they are flying free.

People who have never jumped with ankle harnesses are concerned about the whip that seems to be more severe with an ankle harness than it is with a full body harness. Actually, that appears to be true to an earth-bound spectator, but the jumper would usually not agree. The jumper's entire body is involved in the movement, and the wave of motion comes down the cord, then runs from the feet to the head (Figure 8-1). The human body easily moves with the wave. A bungee site operator can direct the jumper to be as relaxed as possible at the end of each fall. A relaxed jumper will move with the wave easier than a jumper who is tense and fighting against the wave of motion.

The ankle harness is designed to stay on a person's leg even if his shoe were to come off. A high quality harness covers from the ankle to the bottom of the knee. It is held on very tightly with velcro straps and buckles that double back on themselves to keep from working loose. There is enough snug surface contact to hold it in place without putting any pressure on the ankles.

There are some inferior quality harnesses that are very narrow, don't fit tight, and don't have extra secure fasteners (See Figure 1-9).

Some jumps are done with one ankle harness instead of two. While they are usable, they are not as safe as the higher quality harnesses. This does not seem to cause the jumper any more injury than two harnesses. However, the unattached leg has a tendency to go its own direction when the wave of motion travels through the jumper. That can be avoided if the jumper is practiced enough to keep his legs tightly together. If only one harness is used, the redundancy of the bungee system is compromised.

The part of the ankle harness that wraps around the leg is not attached to the bungee cord directly. The harnesses are manufactured with straps of webbing that are about three feet long. Usually there are two straps per harness. This keeps the jumper's ankles and feet away from the hardware at the end of the cord, and makes it easier for him to stand up prior to his leap. (Figure 8-2)

It is recommended that a back-up seat harness or swami belt is used with the ankle harnesses. The seat harness should have attached webbing. Each ankle harness and the seat harness all attach to the bungee cord separately. (Figure 8-3) If they were all hooked into the same carabiner that was in turn attached to the cord, and the carabiner failed, there would be no back-up.

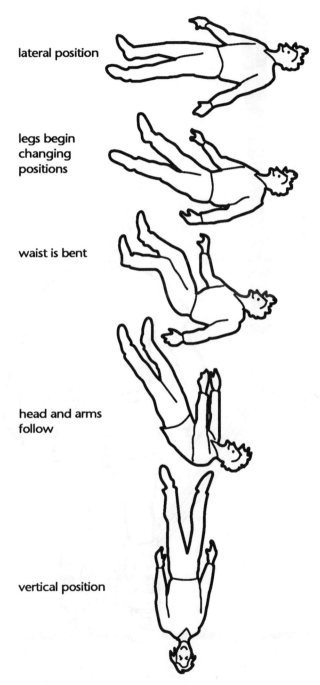

lateral position

legs begin
changing
positions

waist is bent

head and arms
follow

vertical position

Figure 8-1 Wave motion of a jumper's body during a jump.

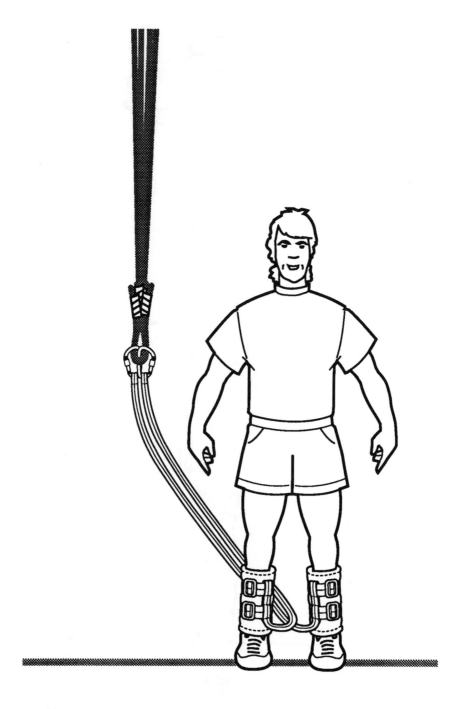

Figure 8-2 Length of ankle harness webbing allows jumper to walk and stand easily.

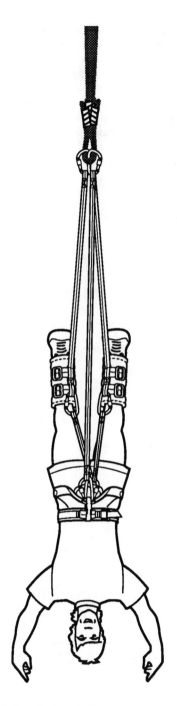

Figure 8-3 Ankle harness attached to a back-up seat harness.

It has been said that the back-up seat harness does not have to be a top quality harness since it is only a back-up. However, if the ankle harnesses fail, the jumper will appreciate a high quality seat harness.

The ankle harnesses present a unique problem to the jumper. At the end of a jump, the jumper will be hanging upside down. It requires a minute or two to retrieve the jumper and by the end of that time, his face will be purple. Also, it is tough to land a jumper when he is head-down. He is swinging in arcs of about twenty or thirty feet, his feet are bound, and he is totally helpless. The crew has to try to carry him until his feet are on the ground. When a two hundred pound person is swinging in a twenty five foot arc, he is an awesome force with which to deal. (Figure 8-4)

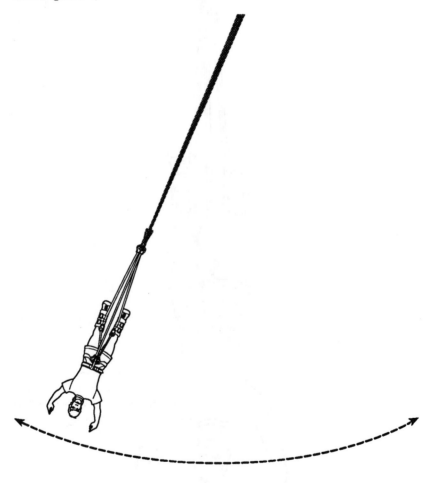

Figure 8-4 Jumper hanging upside down can swing in a 20-30 foot arc with much force.

One answer to this dilemma is to tie one end of a knotted rope to the seat harness and the other end to the bungee cord. The knots on the rope should be bulky and should be placed about every foot along the length of the cord. During one of the rebounds, when the jumper is weightless, he pulls himself upright into a kneeling position with the knotted cord between his legs. He stays in the kneeling position until the time to land is near. As he lands, he stands up and walks away. (Figure 8-5)

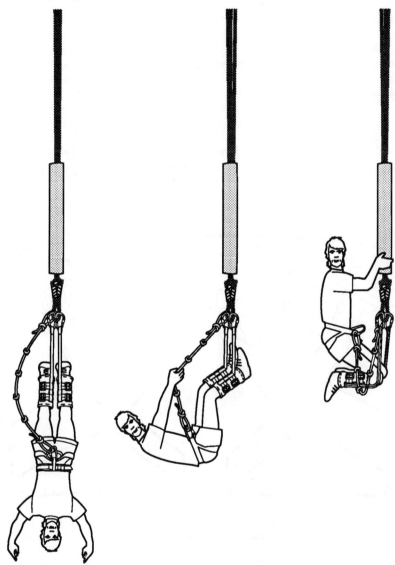

Figure 8-5 Use of knotted rope.

Ankle harnesses are more difficult to obtain than a full body harness because the general market demand for them is less then for the full body harness. However, any mountain climbing shop or bungee jumping system distributor should be able to provide information on where to obtain the harnesses. The most common manufacturer of the ankle harness is Petzl. The Petzl harness is a high quality harness, and is designed for use with a seat harness. The price for Petzl ankle harnesses can run about sixty five to eighty dollars per harness.

Full Body

A full body harness is made up of two parts. It has a seat harness and a chest harness. The two harnesses may be permanently held together, which technically makes them a single unit full body harness. However, the most common configuration is with the two separate harnesses.

There are basically three styles of seat harnesses. A one piece wrap-around uses a continuous loop of webbing for the leg loops and the waist belt (Figure 8-6). A diaper harness have a waist belt, then a second loop pulls up from the back through the legs to form the leg loops (Figure 8-7). The swami belt has a waist belt and then a separate leg loop for each leg (Figure 8-8). The swami belt is the

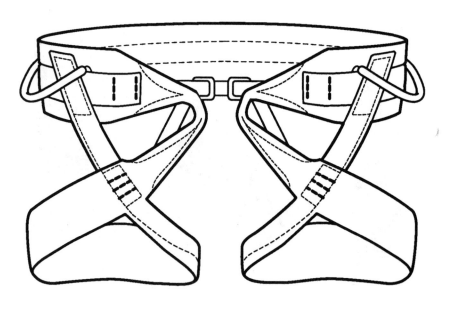

Figure 8-6 Seat harness: Wrap around.

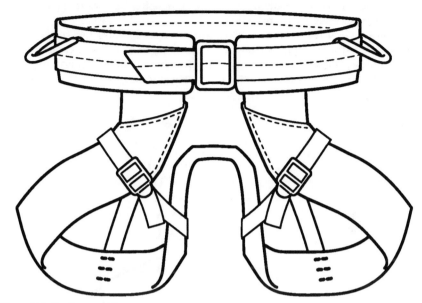

Figure 8-7 Seat harness: Diaper.

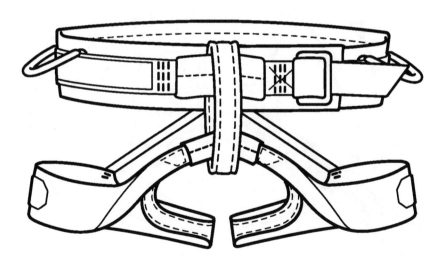

Figure 8-8 Seat harness: Swami belt.

seat harness most commonly used for bungee jumping because it is a heavy-duty harness that is designed for maximum comfort.

Most chest harnesses look like a pair of suspenders attached to a waist belt. The chest harness should be attached to the bungee cords independently of the seat harness. (Figure 8-9) If the connection between the cords and one of the harnesses fails, the second harness is still attached to the cords. The two harnesses

Figure 8-9 Chest and seat harness attached to bungee cord separately.

should also be connected to each other. If the connection between one of the harnesses and the cord fails and that harness falls off the jumper, he will likely fall out of the other harness as well. (Figure 8-10)

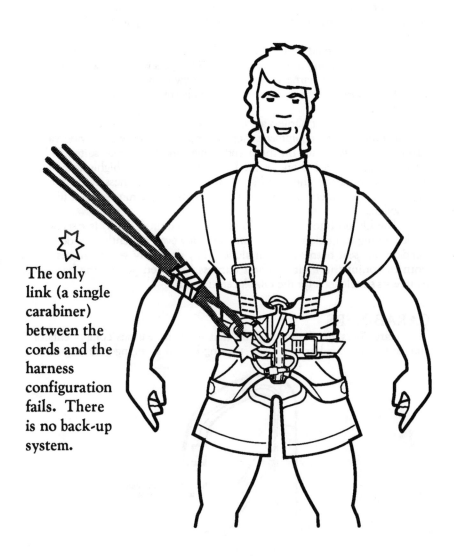

The only link (a single carabiner) between the cords and the harness configuration fails. There is no back-up system.

Figure 8-10 Potential problem with chest and set harness not attached separately to bungee cord.

There is a valid concern about the chest harness causing discomfort to well endowed females, and the seat harness causing discomfort to both males and females. While the harnesses are snug, well endowed females will find that the discomfort from the chest harness is minimal or non-existent, and that they have nothing to worry about with the seat harness since most of the pressure is on the thighs and not the crotch. Guys can have a problem with the seat harness if they are not wearing underwear. Otherwise, the discomfort will be minimal. Either gender may be more comfortable if they wear heavier pants, such as blue jeans vice sweats or shorts.

A jumper should be prepared for the close physical contact that the crew member who is putting the harnesses on the jumpers will have with them during the tightening of the harness. However, the crew member should perform his job with the utmost professionalism, and the embarrassment should be minimal or non-existent.

A seat and chest harness are much easier to purchase than ankle harnesses. Any mountaineering equipment shop will be able to provide a wide variety of harnesses, and guidance on the brand names and styles best suited to bungee jumping. Again, Petzl is one of the best known and most highly recommended manufacturers of the chest and seat harness. A seat harness can run between twenty five and ninety dollars and a chest harness can run between fifteen and sixty dollars.

The Union International Alpinism Association (UIAA) is responsible for implementing regulations for the harnesses. However, presently they do not have standards for seat harnesses worn alone. They do certify seat harnesses that are worn in conjunction with a chest harness.[11] When purchasing harnesses, a bungeeists should look for the UIAA certification.

CARABINERS

Carabiners are the metal links that hold the various components of the bungee system together that have a spring-loaded swinging gate (Figure 8-11).

gate tends to swing shut due to spring tension

Figure 8-11 Spring-loaded swinging gate carabiner.

They can be make out of steel or aluminum. Usually the steel carabiners are used in rescue situations while the aluminum carabiners are used in sports because of their light weight. A carabiner made out of either material is acceptable for use with bungee jumping.

Carabiners come in many shapes. The three most common are oval, three-sided and D-shaped (Figure 8-12). Oval carabiners are not as strong as D-shaped because the D-shaped ones place a larger share of the load to the the longer and stronger side, which is opposite of the gate. The three-sided is designed to handle

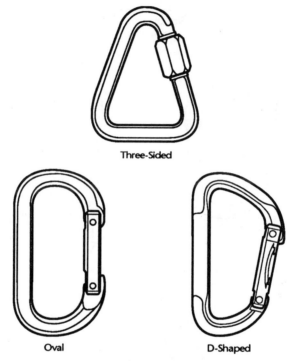

Three-Sided

Oval   D-Shaped

Figure 8-12 Three types of carabiners.

stress that may not be a straight pull, rather multi-directional. On the links where the stress will be in one direction, such as the tether lines on a hot air balloon, the D-shaped are recommended. For stress that is likely to pull in many directions, such as the link that holds all the ends of the cord together and holds a line to a harness (Figure 8-13), the three-sided could be the best choice.

There is a metal link that is similar to a carabiner called a screw link. Often, a screw link is called a carabiner. A screw link (Figure 8-14) is a link that has a screw type gate. The gate is closed by screwing a nut over the opening. The screw link requires more time to open and close, but handles the job as well as a carabiner.

A carabiner can either be a locking or a non-locking carabiner. Non-locking (Figure 8-15) should only be used in non-critical locations, and should

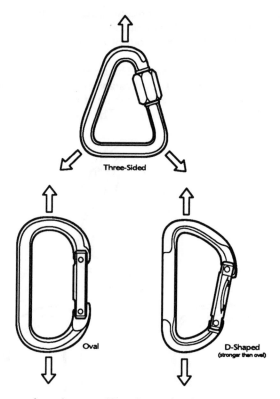

Three-Sided

Oval

D-Shaped
(stronger than oval)

Figure 8-13 Directions of stress best carried by each type of carabiners.

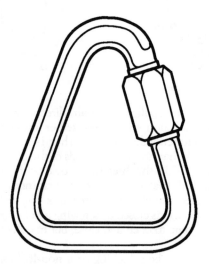

Figure 8-14 Screwlink

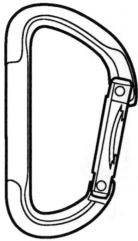

Figure 8-15 Non-locking Carabiner

not be used is situations where they can accidentally be opened. A locking carabiner (Figure 8-16) has a nut that screws over the gate junction.

The load should be carried along the long axis on the carabiner. Otherwise, the stress is carried on the gate, which is the weakest part of the carabiner. (Figure 8-17) The gate is not capable of supporting the weight equal to the breaking strength of the carabiner. Nor is the carabiner capable of supporting weight equal to its breaking strength when the gate is open or unlocked.

If the gate no longer springs shut readily, or the locking screw does not shut easily, that is a sign that the carabiner should be retired. Do not take chances. Carabiners are inexpensive and should be replaced on a regular basis.

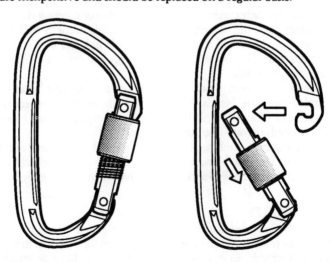

Figure 8-16 Locking Carabiner

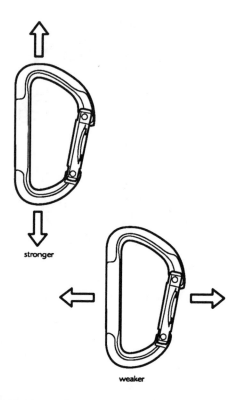

stronger

weaker

Figure 8-17 Best direction of load on carabiner.

More than one carabiner should be used at any one link between components and each carabiner should be capable of carrying the load by itself. If one carabiner fails, the second one provides a full-strength back-up. The life of the jumper should never be supported by a single link any where along the bungee jumping system. The openings of the two carabiners should face opposite directions (Figure 8-18).

The main concern is that a carabiner have a sufficient breaking strength for its intended use. The North American Bungee Association recommends that every carabiner used as a link in the bungee jumping system have a minimum breaking strength of forty five hundred pounds.

Any mountain climbing shop will have a wide assortment of carabiners, and provide guidance on the brand to purchase. Carabiners are priced from a couple of dollars for very small ones to about twenty five for the very heavy large carabiners.

STATIC CORD

Static line or cord is a cylindrical rope (Figure 8-19) with very low stretch, only fifteen to twenty percent at failure. It is used for purposes that require a rope that will not stretch, such as hot air balloon tether lines or attachment of the bungee cords to the bungee platform. It is especially useful in situations where a

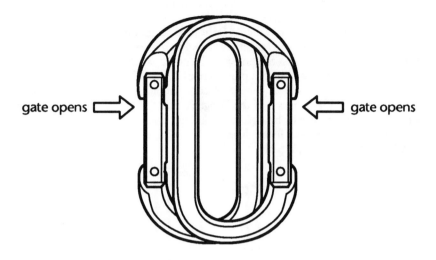

Figure 8-18 Configuration of dual carabiners.

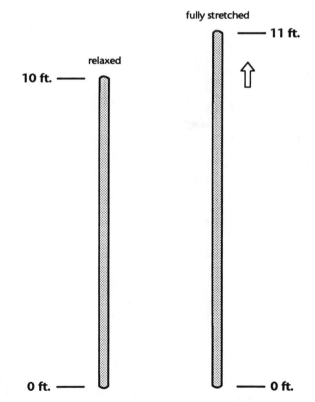

Figure 8-19 Static cord's low stretch.

knot is required as part of the attachment configuration because static cord works well in a knot.

The strength of the cord should be at least seven times the anticipated load if the load is non-critical, such as tether lines. For live loads, the breaking strength of the cord should be at least fifteen times the anticipated load.[12]

If the static cord if used in a prusik knot (Figure 8-20) to attach to a straight bungee cord, the diameter of the static cord should be approximately sixty to eighty percent of the diameter of the bungee cord.[13] If the static cord's diameter is too small, the knot will be tight and difficult to loosen and move along the length of the bungee cord. If the diameter is too large, the knot will be too loose to grab the bungee cord properly.

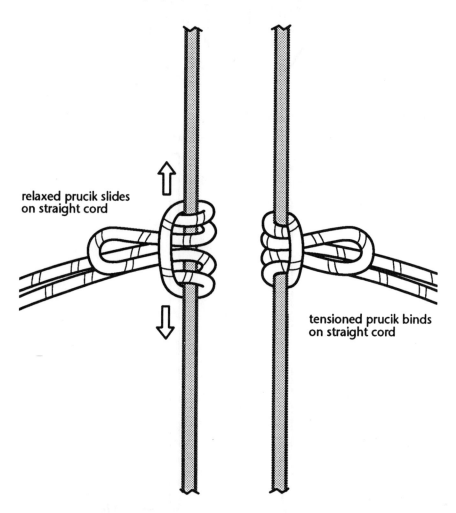

relaxed prucik slides
on straight cord

tensioned prucik binds
on straight cord

Figure 8-20 Allowable movement of prusik knot.

BUNGEE JUMPING

The static line should be inspected at least before and after each day of use, and more often if the cord is exposed to excessive use during any one day. If there are any visible signs of wear, the cord should be retired.

Static line is a common mountain climbing accessory, and any mountain climbing shop will carry the cord.

WEBBING

Webbing is a flat rope that looks like the handles on a gym bag. (Figure 8-21) Its purposes are similar to the static cord, except that it is usually not used in knots, and it is usually used for short runs. It is commonly used between the harnesses and the bungee cords to keep the jumper a few feet away from the cord attachment, or to provide him with a non-elastic "panic handle." It may also be used as a buffer between the bungee cord end eyes and a carabiner that could damage the bungee cords.

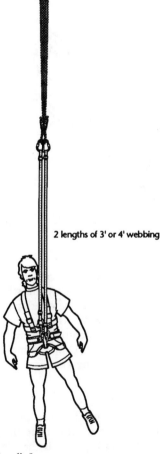

2 lengths of 3' or 4' webbing

Figure 8-21 Webbing used as a "panic handle."

The strength of the webbing should be the same as it is for the static line. For non-critical loads, the breaking strength should be at least seven times the anticipated load. For live or critical load, the breaking strength should be at least fifteen time the anticipated load.[12]

The webbing that is most commonly used in bungee jumping has a breaking strength of 4,000 pounds. Webbing, when employed, is usually doubled as in a sling. Therefore, the breaking strength requirements mentioned above should be met by the total strength of the webbing loop, not necessarily be a single strand of webbing.

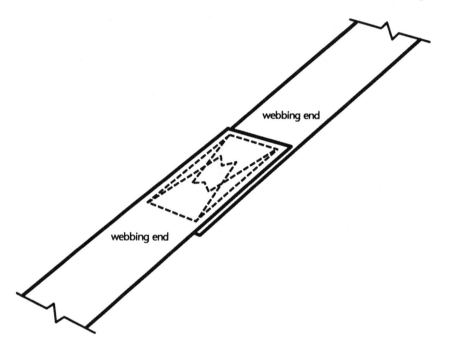

Figure 8-22 "W" stitch.

Webbing is attached to itself to form a loop by stitching. An industrial strength sewing machine is required for this stitching. A standard "W" stitch is a favored stitch. The ends should be overlapped so that they pull in opposite directions. That distributes the strain over all of the stitching rather than focusing it on one end of the stitching. (Figure 8-22)

Once again, webbing is a common mountain climbing accessory and is widely available through climbing shops.

JUMPING SHELVES

The difference between a jumping platform and a jumping shelf is that the platform is the structure to which the bungee system is attached, such as the crane or tower. A jumping shelf is the place on which the jumper stands immediately prior to leaping. The jumping shelf is often referred to as a platform. In order to keep the terms straight, this chapter differentiates between a platform and a shelf.

Each site can have a different jumping shelf. A crane usually has a cage (See Figure 5-1), a hot air balloon can have a little shelf attached to the side of the basket (See Figure 4-3), a bridge can have some kind of diving board attached to the bridge railing (See Figure 3-3).

The distributor of the bungee system often offers a ready made jumping shelf that is designed to interface with their particular bungee system.

The bungee site owner can also design his own shelf. It is wise to involve an engineer because the design of a shelf is not something to take lightly. If the shelf fails, the resulting problems could be fatal.

The jumping shelf should have railings or safety cables that keep the jumper and the jump master from accidentally falling off the platform. The shelf should be easily accessible. A heavy set or short-legged person should be able to comfortably get to the platform, even while being weighted down by the very heavy cords. The jumper should not feel like he is in danger of falling off the platform prematurely.

SAFETY EQUIPMENT

Safety equipment is any accessory that enhances the safety of the crew or of the customers. Helmets, gloves, goggles, life lines, barricades or communication aids are just a few of the pieces of equipment that can be used. It is up to the site owner to determine what equipment is really needed, and what is excess luggage. Gloves can keep the jumper from getting his fingers pinched in the carabiners attached to his harness, goggles can keep a beetle out of his eyes, helmets on the crew can lessen the blow of a wrist watch falling out of a jumper's pocket from one hundred feet.

Any mountain climbing shop, lumber yard or hardware store can provide various equipment pieces. A store employee would be the best bet for gathering information on the particular brands of equipment that they offer.

AIR BAGS

An air bag is a big bag of air that serves to cushion a jumper should his bungee system fail and he falls to the surface (Figure 8-23). An air release system displaces the air when the jumper hits the bag. The bag is commonly used in sky diving training. The bag is rated by the distance a person can fall and still be protected from injury. The ratings run up to about two hundred feet.

Some insurance companies won't insure a site if a bag is not in use. Other insurance companies will give premium reductions if the does use the air bag.

An air bag is far more valuable than a body of water could be. The jumper can fall from one hundred feet into an air bag and walk away absolutely uninjured. If he fell that same distance into a body of water, he likely will have serious injury from the impact.

A manufacturer of military equipment and/or sky diving equipment will either sell the bag or know where one can be purchased. The two bungee associations should be able to provide leads also.

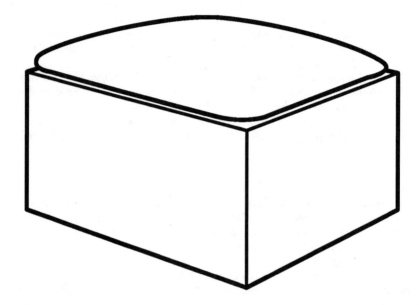

Figure 8-23 Air Bag

Chapter Summary:
Harnesses—Ankle:
- The whip that the jumper experiences from using ankle harnesses is not a violent as it appears to be to an earth-bound spectator.
- There is enough snug surface contact between the ankle harness and the jumper's leg to hold the harness in place without putting any pressure on the ankles.
- It is recommended that a back-up seat harness or swami belt is used with the ankle harnesses.
- A jumper using ankle harnesses needs a way to get back up to an upright position before being retrieved.
- The price for Petzl ankle harnesses can run about sixty five to eighty dollars per harness.

Harnesses—Full Body:
- The swami belt is the style of seat harness most commonly used for bungee jumping.
- Most chest harnesses look like a pair of suspenders attached to a waist belt.

- The chest harness should be attached to the bungee cords independently of the seat harness.
- There are a few hints that can be given to males and well endowed females to avoid physical discomfort.
- A seat harness can run between twenty five and ninety dollars and a chest harness can run between fifteen and sixty dollars.
- The Union International Alpinism Association (UIAA) is responsible for implementing regulations for the harnesses.

Carabiners:
- The three most common shapes of carabiners are oval, three-sided and D-shaped.
- On the links where the stress will be in one direction, the D-shaped are recommended. For stress that is likely to pull in many directions, the three-sided could be the best choice.
- A screw link is a link that has a screw type gate.
- A carabiner can either be a locking or a non-locking carabiner.
- The load should be carried along the long axis on the carabiner.
- If the gate no longer springs shut readily, or the locking screw does not shut easily, that is a sign that the carabiner should be retired.
- More than one carabiner should be used at any link between components and each carabiner should be capable of carrying the load by itself.
- The North American Bungee Association recommends that every carabiner used as a link in the bungee jumping system have a minimum breaking strength of forty five hundred pounds.
- Carabiners are priced from a couple of dollars for very small ones to about twenty five for the very heavy large carabiners.

Static Cord:
- Static cord is used for purposes that require a rope that will not stretch.
- The strength of the cord should be at least seven times the anticipated load if the load is non-critical. For live loads, the breaking strength of the cord should be at least fifteen times the anticipated load.
- If the static cord if used in a prusik knot, the diameter of the static cord should be approximately sixty to eighty percent of the diameter of the bungee cord.
- If there are any visible signs of wear, the cord should be retired.

Webbing:
- The purposes of webbing are similar to the static cord, except that it is usually not used in knots, and it is usually used for short runs.
- The strength of the cord should be at least seven times the anticipated load if the load is non-critical. For live loads, the breaking strength of the cord should be at least fifteen times the anticipated load.
- Webbing is attached to itself to form a loop by stitching.

Jumping Shelves:
- A jumping shelf is the place on which the jumper stands immediately prior to leaping.
- The distributor of the bungee system often offers a ready made jumping shelf that is designed to interface with their particular bungee system.

- The jumping shelf should have railings or safety cables that keep the jumper and the jump master from accidentally falling off the platform.
- The shelf should be easily accessible to the jumper.

Safety Equipment:
- Helmets, gloves, goggles, life lines, barricades or communication aids are just a few pieces of safety equipment.

Air Bags:
- Some insurance companies won't insure a site if a bag is not in use.
- The jumper can fall from one hundred feet into an air bag and walk away absolutely uninjured.

CHAPTER NINE

Training for the Site Operator

It is of utmost importance that a person who is going to open a bungee site, whether it be a commercial site or a private site, obtain qualified training. There are an incredible number of little details that can't be learned through reading a book or watching a video of a jump. The pioneers of the industry went through a trial and error period. They found what works and what doesn't. There is no need to rediscover the basics. Any advancements in the industry should be done with a firm knowledge of the past research.

If a person attempts a bungee jump without the proper training puts himself, his crew, and the reputation of the entire industry in extreme danger. If the bungeeist were to be taken to a court of law, he could be found to be negligent due to his lack of training.

EQUIPMENT

The distributor of the bungee jumping system should have some kind of training program for his consumers. The training should be mandatory so that he can know the users of his equipment will know how to use the system in the safest possible manner. If one of his customers gets involved in a legal battle, the distributor is going to be dragged into the battle as well.

The training may include classroom education as well as hands-on experience at a bungee site that is in operation. The training may only be a day or two in length, or the distributor may insist upon a minimum of two or three weeks of training.

When the customer has completed the training, he should feel confident that he can assemble every single part of the bungee system, including the jumping shelf and retrieving system. He should be able to spot any potential problems with any component of the system. He should know the reasons for the engineering designs of the equipment. He should know what records and logs are necessary to maintain and how to do so. He should know how to coach a customer through the experience. He should know to what laws and regulations the equipment is subject. If the training provided by the distributor does not cover any of those areas, it is the site owner who is responsible for asking questions of either the distributor or another industry expert.

Some distributors are willing to sell the bungee system, or parts of the system without insisting the customer are trained in the use of the equipment. This is especially true if the site owner buys each component of the system separately and designs the configuration himself. In that case, it is again the responsibility of the site owner to obtain the proper training.

OPERATIONAL

The management of the equipment is a very small part of operating a bungee site. The site owner is responsible for making the site run like a well-oiled machine. This part of the management is similar to any small business. A person who has experience in managing a small business might not need much instruction in this area.

The site owner will have a massive struggle on his hands when he begins dealing with the local government. He will have to research and dig to uncover all the hidden permits and regulations that could be thrown in his face the day before his grand opening. Then he has to work through all of the applications and zoning boards and hearings. It has been the general rule of the industry that sites are not well received. Cities are afraid of the negative publicity and traffic problems that could result from the opening of a site.

Talking to someone who has already opened a similar site could help the site owner plow through all the above. While the regulations won't be exactly the same between the two locations, generally the local laws are comparable. The regulations of national regulatory agencies such as the FAA and OSHA will be the same across the country.

An owner of a site that is already in operation could provide guidance on issues such as the best location for the parking lot, the best methods of advertising, how to overcome negative media coverage, what type weather would cause an early closure of the site, how to handle a drunk customer, how to keep the number of "no-shows" down, and what type of "extras," such as tee-shirts and video sell the best. If the mentor site owner is willing, he could provide a hand during the first few days of business. He would know how to handle most of the sticky situations that arise during the first days.

The instruction that a site owner receives from his mentor is not worthwhile if the mentor does not run a high quality site himself. A new site owner may go to a potential mentor's site with the guide from chapter two in his hand. If the mentor's site racks up several brownie points, then he could be a qualified mentor. If his site is less than impressive, his instruction will likely be the same.

A reasonable price for the service of mentorship by someone other than the distributor would run between three and ten thousand. The lower end of the range would feasible if the student site owner provides all the housing, room and board, and all transportation, and the mentor spends a total of three or four days for the effort. The higher number would be normal if the mentor covered all of his own travel expenses and provided some additional equipment such as a few special harnesses or safety equipment and stayed at the site for a week or two to help set up as well as assist with the first few days. It would be expected in any case that the mentor would be available for a few months for phone consultation.

CUSTOMERS AND CREW

The site owner is responsible for making sure the site is a fun place to work and a fun place to visit as a customer. Disgruntled crew members will not perform well, and the customers will not find the jump to be an awesome experience.

Each crew member should know his job inside and out, and should have a solid comprehension of the site operations and equipment. He should be able to answer just about any question that a member of the general public might ask. The crew should handle themselves professionally since the customers are placing their lives in the hands of the crew. The customers will already have some qualms, and an immature crew will not help the situation.

The site owner should know how to command his crew professionally, and he should personally know how to perform the job of every single crew member.

A common practice used in training crew members is to have a new crew member walk in the shadow of a regular crew member. Then the new crew member attempts to handle the responsibility while the regular crew member walks in his shadow.

The crew should be well trained in emergency measures. There should always be one crew member on hand who is trained in first-aid. The crew should know who to call, where to call from and what to say in the event of an emergency.

The customers should be instructed on the site procedures. They should know what is expected of them and when. They should know what style of jumping is to be used, and exactly when they are to jump. They should know important details such as grabbing onto the bungee cord during the jump does not feel good to the arm pits.

A customer should be fully aware that they are not to be under the influence of drugs or alcohol. They should be informed as to what the penalties are for being in that state. The crew should know how to enforce that rule.

Chapter Summary:
Equipment:
- The distributor of the bungee jumping system should have some kind of training program for his consumers.
- The training may include classroom education as well as hands-on experience at a bungee site that is in operation.

- Some distributors are willing to sell the bungee system, or parts of the system without insisting the customer are trained in the use of the equipment.

Operational:

- The site owner will have a massive struggle on his hands when he begins dealing with the local government.
- Talking to someone who has already opened a similar site could help the site owner handle potential problems.
- The instruction that a site owner receives from his mentor is not worthwhile if the mentor does not run a high quality site himself.
- A reasonable price for the service of mentorship by someone other than the distributor would run between three and ten thousand.

Customers and crew:

- Each crew member should know his job inside and out, and should have a solid comprehension of the site operations and equipment.
- The crew should be well trained in emergency measures.
- The customers should be instructed on the site procedures and should know what is expected of them and when.

CHAPTER TEN

Standards

E very industry starts out with a few members who operate by whatever rules they deem appropriate. No one stands over them and enforces a particular standard of safety. When the number of members increases, the original members begin to worry that the new members will not maintain a decent operational and safety standard and will ruin the industry's reputation. To keep that from happening, the original members set standards and try to enforce them across the industry.

This is the story with the bungee jumping industry. In Europe, the New Zealand standards were set, and in the United States, the North American Bungee Association is writing guidelines for the sites in the United States.

NEW ZEALAND/AUSTRALIAN

The company that has been the most involved in writing the New Zealand/Australian standards is A.J. Hackett Bungy based in New Zealand with sites in Australia. They are one of the largest and most respected bungee companies in the world.

The latest version of the proposed standards is a set of three books totaling ninety eight pages that is dated December 1990. From the number of pages in the document, it is obvious that the standards are very detailed. They provide standards for each piece of equipment, the platform and jumping shelf, operations, safety and emergency medical response.

AMERICAN

In early 1991, two separate American associations were working on writing standards for the American sites. The American Bungee Association (ABA) is led by Ricco Nel of Huntington Beach, California. The document put together by the ABA was nearly as large of the New Zealand document, and just as detailed. The bungeeists who were involved in writing that document are very qualified to write the document due to their knowledge of and experienced in the sport of bungee jumping.

The second association was the International Association of Bungee Enthusiasts (IABE), currently known as the North American Bungee Association (NABA). The association was originally led by Nancy Frase of Reston, Virginia, then by John Weinel of Valencia, Pennsylvania, and currently by Thomas Woodard of Park City, Utah. In July of 1991, the two associations joined forces and are further developing what are now called guidelines rather than standards.

Florida and Georgia have adapted the New Zealand standards and made them law for the sites within their state borders. Refer to Appendix C for a copy of the Georgia bungee rules. Several other states have considered the same move, as well as the Department of Labor on a national level. It is the hope of the American associations to convince each state and the nation to accept the American standards as law across the country.

DIFFERENCES BETWEEN THE TWO STANDARDS

One difference is that the New Zealand standards require the jump zone to be located over water. That is not such a problem in Europe where bridge jumping is usually allowed. In the United States, bridge jumping is not allowed in most states, and hot air balloons and towers sites are difficult to operate over water. In addition, air bags have become available to sites and are a better "safety net" than a body of water.

A second difference is that the New Zealand standards encourage the use of a single uncovered bungee cord. It is common belief in the United States that a multi-cord cord system with covered cords is a much more reliable system.

A third difference is that the New Zealand standards encourage the use of ankle harness exclusively. Most sites based in the United States believe that full body harnesses are just as reliable, if not more user-friendly, than the ankle harnesses.

In short, the American associations are not writing new guidelines because they believe the New Zealand standards are inferior. Rather, the standards need to be altered to meet the needs of an industry that is different than the industry for which they were written.

Chapter Summary:

New Zealand/Australian:

- The company that has been the most involved in writing the New Zealand/Australian standards is A.J. Hackett Bungy.

American:
- Two associations, the NABA and the ABA are working together to establish guidelines for the United States industry.
- Two states have adapted the New Zealand standards for use in those states, but the two American associations are trying to change those state's standards to the American guidelines.

Differences Between the Two Standards:
- New Zealand standards require the jump zone to be located over water and the American guidelines do not.
- The American guidelines encourage the use of a multi-cord system while the New Zealand standards encourage the use of a single cord system.
- The New Zealand standards encourage the use of ankles harnesses only and the American guidelines allow use of full body or ankle harnesses.

CHAPTER ELEVEN

Insurance and Liability Issues

Most of the original sites did not carry liability insurance simply because it was not available. Even currently, many sites still do not carry it if they believe that avoiding the insurance payment insurance is worth the risk of loosing a lawsuit. However, most sites do carry insurance. Either they don't want to loose the shirts off their backs, or the land owner, crane owner, or local regulations require that they carry liability insurance.

In addition to liability insurance, there is workman compensation, and insurance on specific equipment that should be considered.

LIABILITY

In the case of a lawsuit, the people and companies that can be sued include anyone who was in the chain of commerce. That means that the manufacturer, distributor, site owner and the person who trained the site owner, land owner, bridge owner (even if it is the government), crane owner, balloon pilot, the government office who provides business permits, crew members and the person who designed the site's tee-shirts are all at risk. The injured party has every right to sue whoever they wish. They may not be able to prove each party responsible, but they do have the right to sue anybody.

A customer may sue because of an obvious injury that is visible at the time of the jump. He may sue over a sore back that becomes sore two months after the jump. He may sue because the shirt he bought from the site caused an allergic reaction on his two-year-old niece who wore it as a nightgown.

INSURANCE

The liability insurance should protect against litigation for damage to property belonging to, or bodily injury to, the spectators, crew, land owner, platform owner and customers due to an incident relating to the jump, site property or souvenirs. The coverage should be at least two million aggregate, which means the total of all claims; and at least one million per incident. It is common for crane owners to demand as much as ten million aggregate before they will lease a crane to anyone. A sample of a liability insurance policy is provided in Appendix D.

In early 1991, it was common to pay a premium of fifteen to twenty percent of gross income in addition to establishing an account that serves as a deductible. The account could not be touched except for the purpose of paying a deductible, and often the account had to maintain a balance of somewhere between ten thousand and two hundred thousand.

Currently, premiums are running between five and fifteen percent of gross and the additional deductible account is either not used or the required balance is under thirty thousand.

To find an underwriter, a site owner can contact either association, the agent shown in Appendix D, or any independent insurance agent who specializes in high-risk adventures.

If a bungee site is using a hot air balloon, they are required to carry a liability insurance policy that is similar to a car's insurance policy. However, if the balloon is used for bungee jumping, there is a good chance that the balloon's insurance policy may be voided. Many underwriters feel that bungee jumping is a high-risk sport and will not cover the balloon. However, if the bungeeist is following the regulations established by the FAA, the underwriter does not have a case to stand on unless a clause that specifically mentions bungee jumping is written into the contract.

A customer's health coverage may be voided when he participates in bungee jumping. Again, this is because bungee jumping may be considered a high-risk sport by the health insurance underwriter. Sometimes the insurance company who provides the liability insurance for the bungee site will provide a supplemental coverage that acts as a temporary health insurance for the customers. This supplemental coverage would cover incidents relating to the bungee jumping. The coverage would not require a lawsuit for the customer to recover medical expenses.

OSHA requires that all paid employees be covered by workman's compensation. The crew members that would not have to be covered are the site owners and volunteer workers.

WAIVERS

The purpose of a wavier is to alert the customer of the risk involved with participating in the sport of bungee jumping. It is also to protect the bungee site in the event of a lawsuit. In a court of law, the waiver can release a bungee site from having to compensate a participant for injury or damage resulting from involvement with a site. If the participant signed their name to a document that stated that they were aware of the potential dangers and that they would not hold the bungee site responsible for any injury or damage resulting from the bungee jump, that document will usually stand up in court.

There are particular phrases and clauses that need to be included in the waiver to make it valid. A lawyer should be intimately involved in the writing of a waiver. Each state has laws that affect the contents of the waiver.

One reason that some waivers do not stand up in court is because the participant states they were not aware of what they were signing, or that they were forced to sign under pressure. A site should take extreme steps to make sure that the participant knows what they are signing, and that there is proof of that knowledge. One possibility is to video tape each customer reading the waiver, initialing each paragraph, and finally signing the bottom line. The videos should be filed away for seven to ten years.

Many sites feel that if a high quality waiver is used for every jump, then a liability insurance is not needed. The waiver is not worth anything if someone finds a loop hole and can shoot down the waiver in court, or if a crew member or the site is found to have been negligent. Negligence can include a crew member smoking pot an hour before he shows up for work. A site manager can't always pick up on a marijuana high.

On the other hand, many sites feel that if insurance is carried, then a waiver is not needed. Since most liability underwriters require the use of waivers, this argument is a trivial one.

Chapter Summary:

Liability:
- In the case of a lawsuit, the people and companies that can be sued include anyone who was in the chain of commerce.

Insurance:
- The liability insurance should protect against litigation for damage to property belonging to, or bodily injury to, the spectators, crew, land owner, platform owner and customers due to an incident relating to the jump, site property or souvenirs.
- Currently, premiums are running between five and fifteen percent of gross income.
- If a balloon is used for bungee jumping, there is a good chance that the balloon's insurance policy may be voided.
- A customer's health coverage may be voided when he participates in bungee jumping.
- OSHA requires that all paid employees be covered by workman's compensation.

Waivers:
- The purpose of a wavier is to alert the customer of the risk involved with participating in the sport of bungee jumping. It is also to protect the bungee site in the event of a lawsuit.
- There are particular phrases and clauses that need to be included in the waiver to make it valid.
- A site should take extreme steps to make sure that the participant knows what they are signing, and that there is proof of that knowledge.
- If a waiver is used at a site, insurance is still needed, and a waiver is still needed if a site has liability insurance.

CHAPTER TWELVE

Injuries

The fear of injury or death is the driving force behind the development of insurance policies, standards, governmental regulations, redundant systems, safety equipment and intense training. It is the greatest fear of a site owner. The best precautionary measures can't guarantee an injury or death won't occur at a site, but they lessen the chance.

This fear of injury or death resides in the minds of the customers as vividly as it does in the minds of the site owners. Some customers prefer to face this fear with humor. That became apparent to the author when she received a message on her answering machine in which a growling voice monotoned, "Aye, aye, aye; aye, aye, aye; jump off the bridge and die; aye, aye, aye; aye, aye, aye; I'm the dead man from the deep; aye, aye, aye." This chapter looks at ways that a site can keep this humorous tune from becoming a deadly truth.

HISTORY

Out of the near three million jumps made world-wide, there have been relatively very few injuries and deaths. To date, there have been five recorded deaths world-wide, and four recorded critical injuries. The incidents have mainly been due to operator error. That doesn't make the incidents any less tragic, it just indicates that improvements need to be made to operational procedures.

CAUSES OF ACCIDENTS

One accident caused by operator error happened when a crew member attempted to pick up a soda can from a person standing on the ground. He jumped from a hot air balloon. The recommended distance that a jumper should be from the ground is one third of the platform height. That ratio is higher than with any other platform because the balloon is a fairly unstable platform. He jumped from ninety eight feet. His clearance should have been a minimum of thirty three feet from the ground. Yet, he planned to come within six feet of the ground. He jumped in a style that was different than normal that caused him to fall further than planned. He hit the ground.

A stuntman planned to perform a bungee jump from a billboard in front of motion cameras. They were running short on daylight, so he did not take the time to test the cords with a sandbag before jumping from them. The cord stretched further than he anticipated, and he hit the ground.

A bungee site instructor was demonstrating to the to-be-jumpers how to do a bungee jump from a hot air balloon. His harnesses were not double and triple checked, and the sling used to connect the two harnesses was not connected properly. During his fall, the sling pulled loose, and the instructor fell to his death.

One of the accidents occurring due to equipment failure happened when one of multiple bungee cords broke during a tandem water-dunk, and the couple hit the water harder than planned. One of them was seriously injured.

A teen-age girl died when one of the straps on her ankle harnesses broke. She had no back-up harnesses attached.

A man fell to the water below when his single-cord system with uncovered cord broke during the first half of his initial fall. If he would have been using a multi-cord system, the faulty cord would have been backed-up by the other cords.

TYPES OF INJURIES

Obviously, major injuries are impact related and usually include severe internal bleeding, ruptured organs, broken bones and head injuries. Minor injuries include pinched fingers, cord burns on hands, limbs or face; sprained, fractured, or broken limbs; and pinch marks.

The minor injuries are caused from getting fingers or skin in between the metal links or solid parts of the equipment, or from the jumper getting hit with the cord, rope or hardware. Protective covering over the joints, and padding over the hard parts of the system that are close to the jumper can protect from injury. Safety equipment can be also very useful in protecting the jumper.

WHAT TO DO IN CASE OF AN ACCIDENT

The first contact that should be made in a serious injury is the emergency medical response team. A 9-1-1 call is in order. The crew members should know prior to the occurrence of an accident how to reach the emergency team. A phone or radio should always be available on the site for that purpose. The crew member who is trained in first aid should begin his rescue efforts.

After the victim has been taken care of on an emergency care basis, the site owner should contact, within twenty four hours, the proper authorities within the local government, the FAA (if appropriate), the insurance underwriter, the site's lawyer and the North American Bungee Association. The names and numbers should have been compiled prior to the accident. As is true with any accident in any industry or situation, the site owner and employees should not sign any papers or admit any guilt unless directed by the site's lawyer.

The biggest challenge for the site owner in the time immediately after an accident will be the handling of the news media. The last thing the site owner will want to do is to have microphones and note pads jammed in his face. He will be emotionally shook up, and in the middle of a whirlwind of action. However, if he ignores the media, they will write the stories based on whatever spectators say, and on whatever little factual data they will know themselves. This usually is very little since bungee jumping is a new sport. If the site owner does respond immediately to the media, he will not have a clear and prepared statement, and he may say something that should not have been said. The best thing to do is to appoint a crew member as the media contact. This member would be appointed long before an accident occurs, and would have a template statement that would provide just enough facts to satisfy the media, and yet control the damage caused by media exposure.

Chapter Summary:
History:
- To date, there have been five recorded deaths world-wide, and four recorded critical injuries.

Causes of Accidents:
- The major of the accidents were caused by operator error, or they might have been avoided if the bungee system would have been redundant at all points.

Types of Injuries:
- Major injuries are usually caused by impact the surface below the jump zone, and minor injuries are usually caused by the jumper coming in contact with some part of the bungee system.

What to Do in Case of an Accident:
- The first contact that should be made in a serious injury is the emergency medical response team.
- The site owner should contact, within twenty four hours, the proper authorities within the local government, the FAA (if appropriate), the insurance underwriter, the site's lawyer and the North American Bungee Association.
- The biggest challenge for the site owner in the time immediately after an accident will be the handling of the news media.

CHAPTER THIRTEEN

Government Regulations

This chapter is about the part of setting up a commercial bungee site that is the most challenging part. Working through the rules and regulations that are set by government agencies is ninety percent of the battle. It is a very frustrating battle, the battle that makes most potential site owners quit before they get started. There is no easy way to plow through the regulations. Many of the regulations have been discussed through out the previous chapters. This chapter will act as a recap of them.

With a hot air balloon, the FAA requires that the balloon is certified as airworthy, that the pilot be licensed as a commercial pilot, that the balloon is tethered during a bungee jump and that any modifications made to the balloon for the purpose of bungee jumping be approved by a FAA inspector or engineer.

OSHA protects the employees of a site by requiring the site to provide workman's compensation, the cage on a crane to have solid sides, a solid floor, a safety gate, to be engineered by a certified engineer and welded by a certified welder; the crane operator to be a certified operator, the crane has an anti-two block brake system and the jump master to be either a volunteer crew member or one of the site owners.

A piece of land used for a commercial venture that serves the public is usually zoned commercially. That often means the site will have to have paved parking, night lighting, direct access to public road, restrooms, documentation on the engineering of the equipment and the site procedures. Furthermore, local regulations may require adherence to building codes, liability insurance, noise control, crowd control, particular acreage and instructional posted signs. A site could be shut down if it is a traffic hazard. The site owner will more than likely have to go before a zoning board with a proposal.

The local government requires that several permits be obtained. The site owner needs to contact the city, county and state governments to find out what permits are required. There may be operational business permits, building permits, noise permits, crowd capacity permits, tax permits, and many more. Some permit applications will have to accompanied by a check to cover some fee, or may require a background check of the site owners.

It is a wise idea to incorporate the entity that owns the site. This can provide some level of protection for the business owners against liability. A business lawyer can provide guidance on what type of corporation is the best. A tax identification number should be obtained before the site opens.

Chapter Summary:
- Working through the rules and regulations that are set by government agencies is ninety percent of the battle of setting up a site.
- The FAA is involved with the use of a hot air balloon, and OSHA is concerned about protecting the employees of any site.
- A piece of land that is being used for a commercial venture that serves the public is usually zoned commercially. There are many rules and regulations that apply to a commercially zoned site.
- The local government will have their own set of rules and regulations that need to be followed.
- It is a wise idea to incorporate the entity that owns the site.

CHAPTER FOURTEEN

Finances, Sales and Marketing

E ach site owner will have his own style of advertising and marketing. He will have his own ideas on what memorabilia will be good sellers. He may keep very minimal financial records, or he may hire a full-time CPA. Whatever his style, there are a few tried and true pointers that he can benefit from knowing.

The price of the jump should be as low as possible. In 1990, there were so few sites that each site could pretty well name whatever price they wanted because there was no competition. People were so excited about finding a site that they would pay any price to be able to jump, even after driving five hundred miles to the site. Because of the growth of the industry, that is no longer true. The price should be set at the minimum amount that can still allow for a profit.

In California, the prices will be lower than in any other part of the country because the competition there is higher than any other state. A typical price would be in the range of forty to eighty dollars. The first jump might include a special seminar, a tee-shirt, or a video tape of the person's first jump. The second jump may cost less and include only the jump.

Some sites make use of the "club" concept. After the first jump, a person can join the site's jump club. The jumper receives a membership card that entitles him to discounted jumps at that site.

First time jumpers usually want something by which to remember their jump. Tee-shirts are hot sure-profit items. Video tapes of the first jump are hot sellers; however, the time, effort and expense required to produce a video costs almost as much as the customer is willing to pay. Bumper stickers are a break-even item. If the site owner can find a snack and soda distributor who is willing to sell the concessions at the wholesale price, food and drinks can turn a fair profit.

If a site is the first bungee site in the general area, the news media will be hot for a story on the site. That media coverage is free advertising and should be used as advantageously as possible. It is the general rule that the media coverage will attract enough customers that additional advertising is rarely needed during the first jumping season.

Other advertising ideas include distributing flyers to sport clubs, colleges, or sky diving sites. Radio ads may cost more money to produce and place than what they are worth. Newspaper ads with a coupon work well since they are not difficult to produce and don't cost much to place. Also, something that is printed and can be cut out tends to be passed around. A radio ad can't be passed hand to hand.

It seems that there is a huge profit to be made from jumping fifty people a day at sixty dollars a jump plus profit made from tee-shirts and other memorabilia. However, take into consideration that the weather can be bad on thirty percent of the planned jump days. Consider that on half of the jump days only twenty two people show up. The entire crew shows up and has to be paid on the days that the customers don't arrive in flocks. Granted, scheduling customers lessen the time the crew stands idle, and insisting on non-refundable deposits lower the number of no-shows. Yet, the lease payment on the crane has to be paid even if only ten jump days can be scheduled instead of the twenty a month that the business plan anticipated.

The expenses that a site owner can expect include the obvious. The crane, balloon, tower or bridge, bungee equipment, crew salaries, insurance, workman's compensation, safety equipment, lawyer fees, business permits, incorporation fees, engineer fees, training expenses, advertising, land and land preparation have all been discussed in previous chapters. Then unexpected expenses that can be added to the list include printing of proposals for the zoning board, propane for hot air balloons, replacement for crane starter motors that burn out from repeated starts, replacement of the equipment trailer when it gets wiped out in an accident, and court fees for a lawsuit involving a wreck that happened when a car drove off the road while watching someone jump.

These words are not to discourage potential site owners. They are meant to force a realization that opening a bungee jumping site will not make a person a millionaire overnight. A solid financial base is needed if a site is to be operated responsibly. It is reasonable to expect a potential site owner to come up with at least one hundred thousand in start-up capital before he ever opens his doors to customers. He has to have the money to operate the site in a training and experimental mode for hundred of jumps before he can open to the public. He is not going to show a profit for at least a month or two, maybe a year or two.

Obtaining that much start-up capital is a challenge with a capitol "C". It is tough to find people who are willing to invest thousands of dollars in some unproven, wild and crazy venture. Banks won't make a loan without collateral, and there is not much collateral in a bungee site unless the site owner just happens to own a crane lien-free. Usually a site is started up by a group of people who love to jump themselves, who believe in the industry, and who plan to have an active part in running the business. Someone who is looking for partners to start a site with might do well to break into the network provided by the North American Bungee Association.

Chapter Summary:
- The price of the jump should be as low as possible.
- Some sites make use of the "club" concept.
- First time jumpers usually want a souvenir by which to remember their jump.
- If a site is the first bungee site in the general area, the news media will be hot for a story on the site.
- While it seems that a bungee site should bring its owner a solid profit, that is not always what happens.
- It is tough to find people who are willing to invest thousands of dollars in a venture they believe to be unproven, wild and crazy.

CHAPTER FIFTEEN

Mentoring a New Site

A person who is well versed on the operation of a bungee site is marketable to another person who is attempting to set up a new site as a mentor. Even beyond being marketable, he is invaluable. He knows how to use the bungee equipment. He has plowed through the unpleasentries, he knows what input that a potential site owner receives from regulatory agencies is accurate and what is pure trash. He knows when to quit and when to keep on keeping on. He can proverbially hold the hand of the new site owner at two o'clock in the morning when the whole project seems doomed.

The mentor can provide his services through a franchise. Another option is to accept a flat fee for advising the new site owner during the set-up and during the first few days of business. I the mentor provides a franchise, he is then entitled to royalties from the income of the new site in addition to an initial down payment.

The advantage of offering a potential site owner a franchise is that the efforts spent in designing the original site can be applied to subsequent sites. The mentoring corporation receives a profitable return their designs and engineering, and the new site owner is able to set up a site with the least hassle, in the least amount of time, and using a proven system. The mentoring corporation can provide advertising brochures, videos, tee-shirts or radio spots for the new site.

The short comings include the large amount of money that the new site owner has to come up with, and the large profit margin he has to maintain in order to cover the royalty payments and still make his efforts worthwhile financially.

Also, a franchise that has been established for many years has a track record that the new site owner can examine, a bungee jumping franchise won't have that lengthy track record. A franchise that is well-established will have a history of financial standing, a bungee jumping franchise will only have a year or two of recorded financial history. It is very easy to manipulate the figures on a balance sheet to make the corporation's standing look better than the true standing. Only a long-term history can expose such discrepancies.

It is considered risky to purchase a franchise from a corporation that only has one product to sell, that is newly established, or that has a near monopoly of the industry. Unfortunately, any bungee jumping franchise will be flagged as risky by those standards. The best bet for a potential franchise purchaser is to talk to other franchise owners.

A mentor has the other option of advising a new site as an independent contractor. He is available for phone consultation as needed, and then when the physical site is being set up, he can travel to the site to assist. Then he is present at the site's opening days of business to work through problems as they arise. He may provide some equipment to the new site.

This arrangement is ideal if the mentor does not want to hassle with the continuing ties and extra paper and legal work that comes with a franchise, and if the new site owner wants to set up his site his own way. The mentor can help the new site owner develop his own ideas.

It is difficult to know if the mentor is qualified as a consultant. If the mentor operates his own site, the new site owner can unobtrusively visit the site and see if it is a quality site. He can talk to other sites that the mentor has assisted.

A price of a franchise would depend on what was offered. A good estimate would be to figure the cost of the same research, development, services and equipment, and double that. The initial down payment plus the royalties expected over the first two years should equal the doubled figure. The price of the independent contract would run between three and ten thousand for just the consulting. All other expenses would be covered by the new site owner.

With either method of mentoring, the mentor can be liable in the event of a lawsuit. There really is no way that a mentor can insure the new site owner will operate his site in the manner that he was instructed. That is the biggest risk of mentoring. The mentor needs to cover his tail-end with a disclaimer in the contract and maybe professional liability insurance.

Chapter Summary:

- A person who is well versed on the operation of a bungee site is marketable to another person who is attempting to set up a new site as a mentor.
- The mentor can provide his services through a franchise.
- Another option is to accept a flat fee for advising the new site owner during the set-up and during the first few days of business.

- There are a few way to find out if the mentor is qualified as a consultant.
- A good estimate for the price of a franchise would be to figure the cost of the same research, development, services and equipment, and double that.
- The price of the independent contract would run between three and ten thousand.
- With either method of mentoring, the mentor can be liable in the event of a lawsuit.

CHAPTER SIXTEEN

The Skill of Jumping

This subject is a fun one. There is more to a bungee jump than one leap and a scream. There is a reason why many people jump time after time.

COMMERCIAL JUMPING

The first time jumper is going to be very nervous. He will want to know specifically how he is suppose to perform the jump. If the site's training is extensive, the jumper will be much more confident than if he only received two minutes of instruction. The jumper should know when he will have a harness put on him, when he is suppose to walk onto the jump zone, on what command he is to step out onto the jumping shelf, and on what command he is to leap. He should be warned about the weight of the cords, instructed to empty his pockets, and taught how to land.

Some sites will allow a first time jumper to jump with either an ankle harness or a full body harness, whichever the jumper wishes to wear. However, it is a more common practice to allow only experienced jumpers to jump with the ankle harnesses due to the need for a cool head to return to an upright position at the end of the jump.

Each site has their preferences as to the style of jump that a first time jumper should use. Some sites instruct the jumper to face forward, others backward. Some say feet first is best while some say a dive clears the jumper of the shelf. The site owner or jump master should do whatever they feel is best.

First time jumper should not be allowed to try flips. That takes some practice. Usually people just want to get through the experience and are not ready to try flips on the first jump.

More important than the style of jump is the placement of the cord prior to the jump. The jumper should be instructed to hold the cord to the side, to the back, or whatever position clears them of the cord during the jump.

STUNTS

Popular stunts include the negative jump, sandbag, soda grab, tandem jump and water dunk. The negative jump is when a group of people hold down a jumper on the ground while the platform, to which the jumper is attached via a bungee cord, is raised. This results in a taut bungee cord. The group of people release the jumper and he is hurdled toward the platform. The danger with this stunt is that it is difficult to predict the path of the jumper and he could hit the platform.

The sandbag involves one jumper wearing the harnesses in a normal fashion. He bear hugs either a sandbag or a second person who is not fastened to the cords in any way. The duo jumps from a platform, and when the cord has reached full extension, the sandbag or second person is dropped to the landing area. This causes the jumper to rebound to a point higher than the platform. This type of jump is not recommended because the path of the jumper is very difficult to predict, and the jumper can easily hit the platform or other hard objects. Also, the sandbag or second person can be torn from the grasp of the jumper prematurely due to the tremendous velocity created by the sandbag or person's inertia. The sandbag or person may land in an undesirable location and injure people on the ground as well as possibly the person who has been dropped.

The soda grab involves a jumper who picks up a soda can from either the ground or from an earth-bound person during a jump. This jump places the jumper closer to the ground than is reasonably safe.

The tandem jump is when two people are attached together and then attached to the bungee cords as if they were one person. The additional risk is minimal with this jump as long as the equipment is set up for the heavier load.

A water dunk places the jumper's head or feet into water at the bottom of the initial fall. This jump removes the cushion of space that should be between the ground and the jumper during the jump. It also exposes the jumper to the possibility of hitting debris in the water.

While these stunts are not recommended at a commercial site, there are stuntmen who work in very controlled situations. These stuntmen and their crew are specially trained to handle the extra risk. They perform these special jumps as professionals.

SHOWS

A fascinating part of the bungee jumping industry is the professional shows that are performed for large audiences. There are only one or two groups who do shows regularly. These performers leap from poles, ceilings or special towers. Their stunts demand perfect timing and form.

To locate one of these shows, the American associations as well as the European bungee companies can provide leads on where they are performing and how to attend a show. If a jumper believes they are qualified to join one of the groups, they should contact a show group and interview for the chance.

COMPETITION

The jumpers who have worked very hard on perfecting their form and style should look into competing in bungee jumping. The North American Bungee Association is putting together a competition in the next few years. It will be based on high diving competition guidelines. There will also be opportunity to perform fun stunts and creative jumps.

Chapter Summary:

Commercial Jumping:

- The first time jumper is going to be very nervous. He will want to know specifically how he is suppose to perform the jump.
- It is a more common practice to allow only experienced jumpers to jump with the ankle harnesses.
- Each site has their preferences as to the style of jump that a first time jumper should use.
- More important than the style of jump is the placement of the cord prior to the jump.

Stunts:

- Popular stunts include the negative jump, sandbag, soda grab, tandem jump and water dunk.
- While stunts are not recommended at a commercial site, there are stuntmen who perform them in very controlled situations.

Shows:

- To locate a bungee jumping show, the American associations as well as the European bungee companies can provide leads on where one is performing and how to attend.

Competition:

- The North American Bungee Association is putting together a competition in the next few years.

CHAPTER SEVENTEEN

Bungee Associations

A s mentioned in chapter ten, a natural development within a new industry is for organizations to develop whose purpose is to regulate the industry. Often, several associations develop and then fad or merge. Often, a new association is initially in turmoil. People fight, agree, leave or take sides. Bungee jumping is not an exception to this rule.

This natural conflict is good. It weeds out the people who are using the association as a platform for their personal benefit. It draws out strong leaders. It forces the purpose of the associations to be redefined and refocused regularly.

AMERICAN ASSOCIATIONS

At least two associations have been founded in the United States. One association is the American Bungee Association (ABA). It is led by Ricco Nel of Huntington Beach, California. The goal of the American Bungee Association is to educate and promote the highest standards of safety in the bungee jumping industry. Each member of the founding group had at least two years of experience in bungee related activities.[14] This group compiled an extensive set of standards.

The second association was originally known as the International Association of Bungee Enthusiasts (IABE). Then in July of 1991, the name was changed to the North American Bungee Association (NABA). The association was originally led by Nancy Frase of Reston, Virginia. The second leader was John Weinel of Valencia, Pennsylvania. The current leader is Thomas Woodard of Park City, Utah.

NORTH AMERICAN BUNGEE ASSOCIATION

The first efforts toward the organization of the NABA was a newsletter known as "Bungee Cords." It was founded in December of 1990 by Nancy Frase. Some of the readers of the newsletter were invited by John Weinel to meet just outside of Pittsburgh, Pennsylvania for a bungee jumping meeting. In March of 1991, ten people met and decided to form the IABE.

The next July, the readership of the newsletter had grown to about seventy, and the attendance at a July IABE meeting was about twenty five people. The attendees were from all over the country. The group decided to change the name to NABA.

The next meeting was held in October, in Park City, Utah. The association member had reached about three hundred and was still growing rapidly.

The association has continued the publication of the newsletter. Also, it has been able to offer a master liability insurance policy to its members. With the cooperation of the ABA, guidelines are being developed for the American industry.

A new activity of the NABA is the tracking and investigation of accidents in the American industry. In the event of a serious accident, a team of engineers are sent from the NABA to the site to assist the government officials in their investigations, to provide the media with technically correct information, to provide a support system for the injured party, the injured party's family and site owner, and to gather statistical data for the industry tracking system.

The NABA offers a subscription to the "Bungee Cords" newsletter for twenty five dollars a year. A commercial membership is also offered This costs $500 annually. It entitles the member to voting rights, a subscription to the newsletter, and participation in any program such as the master insurance program.

Chapter Summary:

American Associations:

- At least two associations have been founded in the United States, the ABA and the NABA.
- North American Bungee Association:
- The first efforts toward the organization of the NABA was a newsletter known as "Bungee Cords."
- In March of 1991, ten people met and decided to form the IABE.
- The next July, the name was changed to NABA.
- It has been able to offer a master liability insurance policy to its members.
- With the cooperation of the ABA, guidelines are being developed for the American industry.
- A new activity of the NABA is the tracking and investigation of accidents in the American industry.
- A subscription to the newsletter and a commercial membership is offered.

Appendix A: October 3, 1990 FAA Memo

The following is a memo issued by the FAA instructing FAA field inspectors to not issue field approvals for hot air balloons that have been modified for the purpose of bungee jumping. For further information, refer to Chapter 4: Using a Hot Air Balloon as a Jumping Platform.

Subject: ACTION: "Bungee Jumping" From Hot Air Balloons

From: Acting Director, Flight Standards Service, AFS-1, US Dept of Transportation, Federal Aviation Administration

To: All Regional Flight Standards Division Managers

Date: October 3, 1990

We have recently received requests for information concerning type design approval requirements for "bungee jumping" from tethered hot air balloons. At this time, there is no guidance available to field inspectors for evaluation of this type of operation. Based on early discussions, some obvious concerns have emerged. Since there are no airworthiness standards applicable for equipment used for such operations, there are no current standards for evaluation and approval of the anchoring system of the bungee cords to the balloon. As a result, any "bungee jumping" operations conducted to date, from a type certified product so modified, may have been in noncompliance with the aircraft's type certificate. The unmeasured stress on the bungee anchoring system, and other unknown factors, may constitute endangerment of life and property if a balloon is used for such operations. Therefore, until further notice, DO NOT—REPEAT—DO NOT issue any type of airworthiness or operational approval for this type of operation or associated equipment. Information or questions may be directed to AFS-800.

This memorandum is being sent via telemail to all FSDO's.

William C. Withycombe for Thomas C. Accardi

Appendix B:
May 30, 1991 FAA
Memo

The following is a memo issued by the FAA instructing FAA field inspectors on how to respond to requests for field approvals for hot air balloons that have been modified for the purpose of bungee jumping. For further information, refer to Chapter 4: Using a Hot Air Balloon as a Jumping Platform.

Subject: INFORMATION: "Bungee Jumping" from Balloons

From: Director, Flight Standards Service, AFS-1

Date: May 30, 1991

Reply to Attn of: Duncan:73827

To: All Regional Flight Standards Division Managers Superintendent,
   FAA Academy, AAC-900
   All Flight Standards District Office Managers

The purpose of this memorandum is to provide guidance to Flight Standards field elements regarding the Federal Aviation Administration's

(FAA) involvement with persons engaged in the thrill-seeking sport called "bungee jumping."

"Bungee jumping" began in Great Britain nearly a decade ago when individuals attached on end of large, strong elasticized or rubberized cords (bungees) to their ankles or torsos. The other end was attached to a tall structure, usually a bridge, then the individuals would leap from the bridge. The participants would adjust the length of the bungee cords so that when stretched to their maximum by the falling body, the cords would keep the individual from striking the ground or surface of the water. Because of the elasticized nature of the bungee cords, the person falls and rebounds repeatedly in increasingly smaller oscillations until finally becoming stationary.

Eventually, this practice spread to the United States, gaining notoriety. Various incidents occurred which caused local and municipal governments to restrict the activity by either passing specific statutes or enacting laws forbidding obstruction of or interference with traffic or road commerce. "Bungee jumpers" then switched to tall buildings or construction cranes, but the activity was again restricted by local jurisdictions for similar reasons.

Recently, persons have been using moored or tethered balloons as a launch platform for "bungee jumping," with the bungee cords hooked to a harness attached to the balloon's gondola. A small platform, from which the person leaps, is also attached to one side of the gondola. The FAA believes that participants in this sport switched to balloons both because of ordinances against the activity and because balloons can be taken to areas away from population centers or away from busy airspace.

When the FAA promulgated and/or amended Federal Aviation Regulations (FAR) Parts 91, General Operating and Flight Rules, and 101, Moored Balloons, Kites, Unmanned Rockets and Unmanned Free Balloons, the FAA did not contemplate the use of balloons as launch platforms for "bungee jumping." Consequently, these FAR have no specific reference to this activity. However, even though "bungee jumping" is a sport activity not regulated by the FAR, the operation of aircraft associated with this activity in U.S. airspace is subject to appropriate FAR, including those requiring continuing airworthiness. Balloon operators who offer their aircraft as launch platforms for "bungee jumping" are still responsible for assuring the continuing airworthiness of the aircraft. For example, any alteration to a type-certificated product, such as drilling holes or bolting or securing hardware to the balloon basket to provide attachment points for bungee cords or launch platforms, should be evaluated to determine whether it is a major change that would require FAA approval, and the owner/operator must provide instructions for the continuing airworthiness of the entire aircraft after alteration.

We have no desire to expend FAA resources on attempts to regulate a sport activity in which person indulge at their own risk. Therefore, Flight Standards inspectors shall not respond to requests for approval, or denial, of "bungee jumping" operations or equipment, such as the bungee cords or launch platforms. The FAA also will not expend inspector resources on specific surveillance of "bungee jumping" activities. However, if the operation of the balloon during the "bungee jumping" activity results in noncompliance with any FAR applicable to the aircraft, pilot, or operator, Flight Standards will investigate in accordance with compliance and enforcement procedures in FAA Orders 8700.1, General Aviation Operations Inspector's Handbook and 2150.3A, Compliance and Enforcement Handbook.

Thomas C. Accardi

Appendix C: Georgia Bungee Jumping Rule

The following is the Georgia state rule on Bungee Jumping. It has been developed from the New Zealand bungee jumping standards. This rule is provided as a sample of state regulation. For more information, refer to Chapter 10: Standards.

Copies of the current Georgia state rules and regulations on bungee jumping may be obtained by contacting Chief of Safety Engineering, Georgia Department of Labor, (404) 656-296. For more information, call the Georgia Department of Labor's Office of Public Relations and Information at (404) 656-3032.

300-8-1
BUNGEE JUMPING
DATE: 10-21-91
Revision: 1

300-8-1-.43 BUNGEE JUMPING: This rule specifies and gives guidance on the site, design, testing of equipment, management of the operation, operating procedures, emergency provisions, and procedures for Bungee Jumping. This rule applies to Permanent Facilities only. Bungee Jumping from Mobile Facilities is prohibited. This rule is applicable to all operators of bungee jumping whether for demonstration, or public use.

300-8-1-.44 DEFINITIONS—The definitions in Georgia Statute, 34-12-2 and Chapter 300-8-1-.01, of the Georgia Rules will apply and in addition the following shall apply:

1. AIR BAG—A device which cradles the body and which uses an air release breather system to dissipate the energy due to a fall, thereby allowing the person to land without an abrupt stop or bounce.

2. BINDING OF CORD—Material used to hold the bungee cord threads in place.

3. BUNGEE CATAPULTING—The jumper is held on the ground while the bungee cord is stretched. When the jumper is released, he/she is propelled upwards. BUNGEE CATAPULTING IS PROHIBITED.

4. BUNGEE CORD—The elastic rope to which the jumper is attached. It lengthens and shortens and thus produces the bouncing action.

5. BUNGEE JUMP—When a person free falls from a height and the descent is limited by attachment to the bungee cord.

6. CONTINUOUS OPERATION—Operating for at least two (2) days in a week for more than thirty-six (36) weeks in a twelve (12) month period.

7. CORD—See Bungee Cord

8. DEFINED AREA—The area designated for the bungee jump by the owner or operator.

9. DYNAMIC LOADING—The load placed on the rigging and attachments by the initial free fall of the jumper and the bouncing movements of the jumper.

10. EQUIPMENT—Power or manually operated devices to raise, lower and hold loads.

11. FENCE—A permanent or temporary structure designed and constructed to restrict people, animals and objects from entering the designated bungee jumping area.

12. INCIDENT—An event that results in injury to a person, or an event that causes damage or loss of process (jumping interrupted or stopped).

13. JUMP AREA—The maximum designed area in all directions for the movement of the jumper.

14. JUMP DIRECTION—(Forward or Backward) The direction in which a jumper jumps upon leaving the platform from the jump point.

15. JUMP HEIGHT—The distance from the jump platform to the bottom of the jump zone.

16. JUMP MASTER—A person who has responsibility for the bungee jumping operation and who prepares the jumper for the actual jump.

17. JUMP OPERATOR—A person who assists the jump master to prepare a jumper for jumping and operates the lowering system.

18. JUMP POINT—The position from which the jumper leaves the platform.

19. JUMPER—The person who falls or jumps from a height attached to a bungee cord.

20. JUMPER SAFETY HARNESS—An assembly to be worn by a jumper, which is attached to a bungee cord.

21. JUMPER WEIGHT—The weight of the jumper only, determined by the jump master on a calibrated scale, traceable to a National Standard.

22. LANDING AREA—The surface area of a pad, air bag or water directly under where the jumper lands.

23. LATERAL DIRECTION—The area measured at 90 degrees to the designed jump direction.

24. LOWERING SYSTEM—Any manual or mechanical equipment capable of lowering a jumper to the designated landing area.

25. LOADED LENGTH—The length of the bungee cord when extended to its fullest designed length.

26. OPERATING MANUAL—The document containing the procedures and forms for the operation of all bungee jumping activities and equipment.

27. PERMANENT-PLATFORM—The area attached to a high structure from which jumper falls or jumps.

28. PLATFORM-CATAPULT—PLATFORM CATAPULTING IS PROHIBITED.

29. PREPARATION AREA—The preparation area is separate from the jump area.

30. RIGGING SYSTEM—The bungee cord plus any webbing or rope connected to the bungee cord which is of variable lengths set by the jump master for each jumper.

31. RECOVERY AREA—An area next to the landing area, where the jumper may recover from the jump before returning to the public area.

32. SAFE WORKING LOAD (SWL)—The maximum rated load as determined by the manufacture which can be safely handled under specified conditions, by a machine, equipment or component of the rigging system.

33. SAFETY BELT—A belt designed to fit around the waist of a person which can be attached to either an anchor point or a safety line.

34. SAFETY HARNESS—An assembly to be worn by an operator. It is designed to be attached to a safety line and prevent the jump site operator from falling.

35. SAFETY HOOK—A hook with a latch to prevent rigging or loads from accidentally slipping off the hook.

36. SAFETY LINE—A line used to connect a safety harness or belt to an anchor point.

37. SAFETY SPACE—A space extending beyond the jump zone as a safety factor.

38. STRUCTURE—A permanent tower used for bungee jumping.

39. TESTING AUTHORITY—An organization acceptable to the department for the purpose of testing the performance of bungee cords.

40. UNLOADED LENGTH—The length of the bungee cord laid on a horizontal flat surface without load or stress applied.

300-8-1-.45 SITE AND OPERATING APPROVAL

1. The operator shall obtain a permit from the Department of Labor, Safety Engineering Section to operate on the site. Each permit shall be renewed annually.

2. Site Plan and Equipment Design and Construction:

    a. A report shall contain site plans, safety zones, drawings and specifications of equipment and structures which shall be submitted to the department prior to construction.

    b. Inspections shall be conducted at the discretion of the department.

3. The owner shall provide a certificate of insurance to the department covering any spectator, and any patron in bungee jumping in the amount of one million dollars ($1,000,000.00) per occurrence.

4. Owners shall maintain a safety space of at least sixty (60) inches above the air bag or water surface provided the depth of water is less than nine (9) feet and a side safety space of at least twenty (20) feet in all directions to any structure or mooring lines. However, if the depth of water is greater than nine (9) feet, no safety space is needed.

300-8-1-.46 PERMANENT PLATFORM

1. The Safe Working Load (SWL) shall be determined by the maximum weight on the platform at any one time, with a safety factor of not less than six (6).

2. When the platform is not an integral part of the structure, the attachment devices and the part of the structure to which they are attached, shall have a safety factor of at least six (6) over the total load.

3. The platform shall have a non-slip surface.

4. The platform shall have anchor points for safety harnesses, designed and placed to best suit the operator's movements.

5. The platform shall be fitted with a permanent fence separate from the jump point to contain the jumper during preparation.

6. There shall be a gate across the jump point which shall remain closed when a jumper is not present.

7. The jump master shall stop the jumping operation when the wind speed affects the safe operations on the jump platform and/or the recovery area.

300-8-1-.47 LOWERING SYSTEM

1. The system for lowering the jumper to the landing pad shall be operated by either the jump operator or jump master.

2. There shall be an alternative method of jumper recovery should the main lowering system fail.

300-8-1-.48 BUNGEE CORD REQUIREMENTS

1. The unloaded length of the bungee cord shall be less than one-half (1/2) the designed extended length.

2. The cord shall stretch in the jump to at least 2.5 times its unloaded length in the designed jumper weight range.

3. The operating length of a bungee cord at its maximum designed dynamic load shall not exceed four (4) times its unloaded length.

4. The cord material shall be used according to the manufacturer's recommendations.

5. The cord and its non-metallic connectors shall be destroyed when one of the following conditions occur:

    a. Exposure to daylight exceeds 250 hours. This does not apply when the cord cover or sleeve fully protects all of the cord from visible and ultra-violet exposure.

    b. Six (6) months from the date of manufacture.

    c. Evidence of threads exhibiting wear, such as bunched threads, uneven tension between threads or thread bands.

d. Broken threads in excess of 5%.

e. After contact with solvents, corrosive or abrasive substances.

f. Any other flaws found.

g. As the bungee cord stretches over the course of its jump life, the dynamic load required to extend the bungee to four (4) times its unloaded length will reduce. When this dynamic load reduces to less than the maximum designed dynamic load, the cord shall be destroyed.

6. Bungee cords must be tested daily. Before starting the day's operations, the jump master shall visually inspect the entire length and circumference of the bungee cord for signs of wear. The inspection shall be repeated at least four (4) times during daily operation and recorded in the site log.

a. When unexpected changes in bungee cord performance occur, the bungee cord is to be replaced immediately. The bungee cord shall be subjected to inspection and testing as required in these regulations.

300-8-1-.49 JUMP SAFETY HARNESS AND ANKLE STRAPPING

1. A jump safety harness shall be either a full body harness, a sit harness with shoulder straps or an ankle harness.

2. A jump safety harness shall be available to fit the range of patron sizes accepted for jumping.

300-8-1-.50 ROPES

1. All ropes for holding and/or lowering the jumper shall have a breaking load of at least 4,400 pounds.

300-8-1-.51 HARDWARE

1. Carabiners shall be the screw gate type with at least a minimum breaking load of 4,400 pounds.

2. Pulleys and shackles shall have a minimum breaking load of at least 4,400 pounds.

3. All pulleys shall be compatible with the rope size.

4. Webbing shall be flat or tubular mountaineering webbing or equivalent with a minimum breaking load of at least 4,400 pounds.

300-8-1-.52 TESTING AND INSPECTION

1. All jump rigging, harnesses, lowering system and safety gear shall be regularly inspected and tested as set forth in the operating manual. Inspections, findings and corrective action shall be recorded in the site log.

2. Hardware subject to abnormal loadings, impacts against hard surfaces or having surface damage, shall be replaced.

3. All ropes, webbing and bindings shall be inspected visually, and by feel for signs of wear, fraying, or damage by corrosive substances in accordance with the operating manual.

300-8-1-.53 REPLACEMENT OF RIGGING AND EQUIPMENT

1. Replacement equipment for the following items shall always be available on site:

a. Bungee cords;
b. All ropes;
c. Rigging hardware;
d. Binding, ankle strapping for jumpers;
e. Body safety harness;
f. Life lines and clips.

2. Items of equipment, rigging or personal protective equipment found to be sub-standard shall be replaced immediately.

3. Jumping shall cease immediately when a sub-standard item cannot be replaced.

300-8-1-.54 IDENTIFICATION OF EQUIPMENT, RIGGING, BUNGEE CORD AND SAFETY EQUIPMENT

1. Each item shall have its own permanent identification number.

2. The identification shall not harm the material.

3. The identification shall be clearly visible to the operators during daily operations.

4. The identification of each piece of equipment shall be recorded in the equipment log.

5. The cords shall be color coded as described in the operations manual.

300-8-1-.55 LANDING/RECOVERY AREA INCLUDING THE AREA IMMEDIATELY UNDER THE JUMP SPACE

1. The following requirements shall apply where the jump space and/or landing area is over land:

a. The jumper shall be lowered onto an air bag or clean, smooth, padded surface adjacent to air bag or water. The air bag shall be rated for the maximum free fall height possible from the platform during operation.

b. The landing area shall be free of spectators at all times.

c. The area shall be free of any equipment or staff when a jumper is being prepared on the jump platform and until the bungee cord is at its static extended state.

d. The air bag shall be in position before jumper preparation commences on the platform.

e. A place to sit and recover should be provided close to, but outside the landing area.

f. The landing pad shall be at least 10 feet by 10 feet.

2. The following requirements shall apply where the jump space and/or landing area is over water:

a. The landing and recovery vessel shall be positioned to recover jumpers.

b. The landing vessel shall have a landing pad size at least five (5) feet by five (5) feet.

c. A landing pad shall be placed within the vessel.

d. One person may operate the landing vessel when the vessel is positioned without the use of power. A separate person shall pilot the vessel when power is required to maneuver into and/or hold the landing position.

e. The vessel shall be equipped with Coast Guard approved life jackets and rescue equipment. The landing/recovery operators shall wear required life jackets.

f. The jump space and/or landing area shall be free of other vessels, floating, submerged objects, the public, and any spectators. When the landing vessel is in open waters, it shall be defined by the deployment of buoys. A sign of appropriate size which read "BUNGEE JUMPING—KEEP CLEAR" shall be attached to the four (4) sides of the landing vessel;

g. When the landing area is part of a constructed swimming pool complex or is specially constructed for bungee jumping the following shall apply:

The pool size shall meet the requirements for jump space as designated by the operating manual. Rescue equipment shall be available and the jump space and landing area shall be secured. Only the operators of the bungee jump shall be within the jump space and landing areas.

3. Fences shall be designed and constructed to retain people, animals and objects outside the landing area. A four (4) inch sphere shall not be able to pass through any section of the fence or gate.

300-8-1-.56 JUMP PROCEDURES

1. Adequate storage shall be provided to protect equipment from physical, chemical and ultra-violet ray damage. The storage area shall be secured against unauthorized entry.

2. There shall be a public address system in operation during all hours of business. There shall be a radio communication link on permanent platform sites between the platform and the landing/recovery area or vessel.

3. All staff shall be easily identified.

4. Instructions to jumpers shall be placed at the entrance to the site.

5. There shall be a means of communication to local emergency services within two hundred (200) feet of the operation.

6. Owner(s) shall allow jumps only under the direct control of a jump master.

7. Adjustments for the weight of each jumper shall be made by the jump master's selection of bungee cord and length of webbing or rope attached to the bungee cord.

8. A sign shall be erected listing the medical and age restrictions for jumpers. The sign shall be clearly visible.

9. Any jumpers, in the opinion of the operation's staff, represent a danger to themselves or others shall not be allowed to jump.

10. Jumpers in a visibly intoxicated state shall not be allowed to jump.

11. The minimum age for jumping shall be eighteen (18) years old.

12. Persons between sixteen (16) and eighteen (18) years of age may be allowed to jump with written parental consent.

13. Jumper preparation shall include: harness or binding attachment; instructions to the jumper; landing, lowering, and recovery procedures; return of jumper to the public area; and retrieval of the bungee cord to the platform or its storage position.

14. At the end of each day's operation, the following close down procedures shall be performed: cleaning, inspection, and storage of equipment; and record retention.

300-8-1-.57 SAFETY AND LOSS CONTROL MANAGEMENT

1. A jump master shall be designated Safety, Health and Loss Control

Coordinator. He/she shall hold a first aid rating or its equivalent as required by Chapter 300-8-1-.39 and 300-8-2-.11 of the Rules.

2. Training shall be provided to all staff relative to their duties in the operation team. A record of training shall be available on site for review by the department.

3. A comprehensive emergency plan shall be developed, practiced, maintained and posted at the site entrance.

4. The operating manual shall contain the site rules concerning the health and safety of employees and the public.

300-8-1-.58 INJURY AND DAMAGE

1. All serious injuries shall be reported to the Department within one (1) hour, and the device shall be closed until the Department reopens it. All injuries shall be reported within twenty-four (24) hours to the Department.

2. The site owner shall record all injuries, damage or incidents in the daily log.

300-8-1-.59 STAFF AND DUTIES

1. The minimum age for Jump Master shall be twenty-five (25) years and twenty-one (21) years for other staff members.

2. The staff of a bungee jumping operation shall include at least four (4) persons, with the following roles:

   a. Jump Master: The designated jump master shall have control over the operation and is responsible and accountable for the operation of the site. The person with complete control when jumping occurs. A jump master is the only person who takes the jumper through the final stages of preparation to the jump take-off. The jump master responsible for the training of other staff and shall have a thorough knowledge of the site, equipment, procedures and staff. The jump master is responsible for checking selection of the bungee cord and adjusting the rigging at each jump platform.

   b. Jump Operator: The jump operator assists the jump master to prepare the jumper; assists the jumper into harnesses, safety belts, etc.; attaches the jumper to rigging; operates the lowering system; may carry out landing/recovery operator duties; and assists in controlling the public.

   c. A landing/recovery operator for each landing area: A landing/recovery operator's duties includes assisting the jumper to land on the landing pad or air bag; assisting the jumper to the recovery area; and assisting in controlling the public.

   d. Registration Clerk: Registration clerk's duties include: registration of the jumper; weighing of the jump. An accurate scale shall be used and calibrated three (3) times each year as a minimum, or when in doubt as to accuracy. Controls movement of jumpers to jump platform; controls or assists in controlling the public;

   e. Vessel Operator: The vessel operator's duties shall include operating the landing and/or emergency vessels.

   f. Minimum qualifications for each position on the operating team shall be described in the Operations Manual.

g. Training shall be conducted by, or under the direct supervision of a jump master.

h. Staff who are in training shall be directly supervised at all times.

300-8-1-.60 SITE OPERATING MANUAL AND DOCUMENTATION:

1. Each site shall have an operating manual for the safe operation of bungee jumping. The manual shall be available to the Department.

2. The manual shall include the following at a minimum: site plan; description of operating systems and equipment; job procedures for each task in the operating system; job descriptions for each employee. Personnel qualifications; staff selection procedures; maintenance standards and procedures, testing procedures and recording, criteria for the periodic replacement of rigging, criteria for the regular planned inspections of ropes, webbings, and bindings, emergency plan and procedures, reporting of injuries, damage and incidents. Daily logs regarding information on the site; equipment and rigging, personnel, and bungee cord used, inspection procedures, standards and follow up actions; examples of forms to be used.

3. Daily Pre-opening Operating Procedures which include inspection, testing and checking of the following:

   a. Personal protective equipment including gloves, life jackets, buoyancy aids, harnesses and life lines;

   b. Communication system(s);

   c. New equipment;

4. Staff briefing for the day's operations. Includes assignment of the designated jump master where more than one jump master is on site.

   a. Registration information on jumpers include: Name, address, city, county, state, zip code and telephone number; medical factors and exclusions; age; weight and markings; prepare bungee cord and adjust connections; connect the jumper and check connections to the rigging; and final inspection by jump master and removal of loose objects.

300-8-1-.61 EMERGENCY PROVISIONS AND PROCEDURES

1. Each site shall have and emergency plan.

2. A medium first aid kit, stretcher, back board and blankets shall be maintained on site.

3. All jump masters shall have current first aid certification and complete an annual refresher course.

4. At sites where the jump or recovery is over water, the jump master and all landing/recovery staff shall be holders of a current Life Saving Certificate and shall have passed the equivalent for "in-water rescue of spinal injuries or unconscious patients".

5. Where the site includes moving water or swift water, the site operating manual shall specify the rescue training and/or qualifications required for all operators and staff on the site.

6. Emergency Lighting shall be provided at all jump sites that operate one-half (1/2) hour prior to sun set until one-half (1/2) hour after sun rise. The emergency lighting system shall illuminate the jump platform, the jump space and the landing area. The emergency lighting system shall have its own power source.

Appendix D: Sample of Insurance Policy

An insurance program proposal was submitted to the North American Bungee Association (NABA) on August 23, 1991 by Joseph P. Hatch, Inc. on behalf of Frontier Insurance Company. The NABA approved the proposal and qualified members of the NABA were able to receive coverage. The following is the proposal as submitted. It is provided for the readers' enlightenment on what may be involved in an insurance agreement. It is not intended as a promotion for the aforementioned company. Please note that the policy is subject to change.

PREFACE

It is with great pleasure that we submit to the board of directors of the North American Bungee Association this proposal of insurance. This insurance is designed to provide for the needs of the membership of the North American Bungee Association engaged in the commercial bungee jumping enterprise. The insurance program is being provided by the Frontier Insurance Company located in Monticello, New York. Coverage will be written on a master insurance policy issued to the association. Individual certificates of insurance will be issued in the name of the individual commercial operators who elect to select this insurance.

COVERAGE
The insurance program will provide for the property, equipment and general liability for the respective operators. The general liability policy will provide protection against litigation for bodily injury and property damage arising out of the commercial bungee operations of the membership. Coverage includes, but is not limited to participants as well as spectators liability and the sale of memorabilia, etc. Limits of liability are on a primary bases: $2,000,000 general aggregate; $2,000,000 products and completed operations aggregate; $1,000,000 occurrence limit under ISO simplification. The coverage form is comprehensive general liability subject to standardized, approved exclusions. The policy includes the application which is secured at the time of binding and voids the policy in the event of fraudulent and intentionally misrepresented information. This application must be signed by each member of the association and warrants that each member is in compliance with underwriting and program criteria for the master policy.

PREMIUM
Each commercial member electing to obtain insurance through the master policy of North American Bungee Association will be required to submit a deposit premium equal to $5,000 for each permanent site. For non-permanent sites, a deposit of $5,000 per platform, in use, will be required. In addition to the deposit, a $500 one-time site inspection fee will be required for each permanent site utilized by the operator. For temporary sites, it will be necessary to inspect only one of their sites which will require the $500 inspection fee.

Each insured will submit, at the end of each business week (Friday), all waivers of responsibility (see below) along with a check representing 15% of the gross receipts of the bungee jumps represented by the waivers of responsibility. During the 12th month of operation, the insured may use the $5,000 deposit for the payment of the waivers issued during the 12th month, the coverage will be renewed without any further deposits and in consideration of the waivers and the 15% premium payment.

ELIGIBILITY
The eligibility requirement to become insured under the master policy are as follows:

A. Association membership—copy of certificate of commercial membership
B. Complete site plan and diagram of site
C. Submission of formal operations procedure guidelines
D. Deposit of $5,500 for each permanent site—if not permanent site, a $5,000 deposit per platform as well as one $500 inspection fee
E. Weekly submission of waivers properly executed an signed by participants
F. Weekly submission of premium attached to the waivers
G. Full compliance with underwriting and program criteria

WAIVERS

All waivers used must be those waivers approved by the Frontier Insurance Company and obtained through the offices of Joseph P. Hatch, Inc. Each waiver must include: name and address of participant; whom to contact in case of emergency; acknowledgment of risk section; acceptance of risk; statement of physical and mental fitness; release section. The waivers will include social security number of participant as well as the numbered cord(s) which were used by the participant.

This insurance program is being written on a dividend paying basis. At the end of the third year, the insurance company will evaluate all premiums received as well as losses paid. If profitable, the company will declare a dividend which will be made payable to the North American Bungee Association to disperse as the Board of Directors desires.

CONCLUSION

We hereby respectfully submit this proposal for insurance for approval by the board of directors of the North American Bungee Association. Upon its approval, and confirmation to this office of such approval, the master policy will be placed in full force and effect and made available to the membership of the North American Bungee Association.

Joseph P. Hatch, Inc. hereby makes formal request to the North American Bungee Association's Board of Directors to assume responsibility for the association's membership insurance to be effective immediately. It is with great sincerity that we extend our appreciation for the privilege of providing the association with this proposal.

Respectfully Submitted,
Joseph P. Hatch, Inc.

Endnotes

1 Howe, "Elastic enjoyment: Bungee jumping in KC," p. E-1.

2 Finocchiaro, computerized trajectory analysis.

3 Bungee Cords, vol. 1, no. 9, October 1991, p. 7-9.

4 Federal Aviation Regulations (FAR), FAR 91.13, FAR 91.407.

5 Military Specification MIL-C-5651D, p. 1.

6 p. 16.

7 p. 16.

8 p. 4.

9 p. 16.

10 p. 10.

11 Raleigh, "Tie Into Something Comfortable: Harnesses for All Types of Climbing," p. 95.

12 Weinel, Rock-N-Rescue catalog, p. 91.

13 p. 1.

14 American Bungee Association informational cover sheet.

Glossary

ABA—(see American Bungee Association)

age—the condition of a piece of equipment or the number of times it has been used.

aggregate—(see general aggregate, products aggregate, or completed operations aggregate)

air bag—a device which cradles the body and which uses an air release breather system to dissipate the energy due to a fall, thereby allowing the person to land without an abrupt stop or bounce.

airworthiness—the condition of an aircraft fit and safe for flight.

airworthiness approval—(see field approval)

altimeter—an instrument used to measure altitude.

altitude—the height of an object relative to sea level.

American Bungee Association—the bungee association that is led by Ricco Nel.

American Guidelines—the industry guidelines that are being created by the NABA and the ABA.

anchor point—the location to which one component is attached to another component, usually indicates that the first component is unstable until attached to the second component.

anchoring system—the hardware used to attach the bungee system to the platform or the platform to the ground.

ankle harness—a band or sheet of cloth that wraps around the ankle of a jumper. The harness is held in place by velcro, buckles, and/or straps and is used to attach a bungee jumper to bungee cords. The harness may be used alone, or in conjunction with another ankle harness attached to the jumper's other leg.

ankle strapping—(see ankle harness)

anti-two block brake—a safety feature on a crane that uses a smaller ball with a brake switch to keep the headache ball from coming in contact with the jib, which can cause the cables to be jammed or may unexpectedly pull the jib upwards.

association—an organization that represents a group of people involved in a common activity.

attachment points—the location on a bungee jumping platform to which the bungee jumping system is attached.

back dive—a style of bungee jumping in which the jumper faces the jumping platform and then falls backward and headfirst.

background check—a procedure in which an agency investigates the integrity of a person by examining their personal history. It is common to check the background of a person applying for a business permit.

BASE jumping—a sport that is often confused with bungee jumping in which the jumper wears a parachute that open immediately after the jumper leaps from a bridge. A bungee cord is not used and the jumper's weight is not supported by the bridge.

basket—(see gondola)

binding, cord—material used to hold the bungee cord threads in place.

body weight—the mass of a bungee jumper. The jumper's body weight is one factor used when figuring the force produced during a bungee jump.

boom—the part of a construction crane that extends outward and/or upward and to which the bungee jumping system is attached.

breaking load—(see breaking strength)

breaking strength—a rating that is given to various components of the bungee system, such as the cords and carabiners, that indicates the stress the component is capable of supporting.

bridge—a structure that is built to allow vehicles or people to pass over terrain that would otherwise be difficult to pass over.

buckle—a piece of hardware that is used to hold tightly shut a harness or other piece of equipment.

bumper—a padding that is placed over the few feet of bungee cord that is closest to the jumper. The bumper helps protect the jumper from injury caused by coming in contact with the cord.

bunching—a condition of a bungee cord when either the rubber or the covering gathers together in little bumps and valleys as a result of damage to the cord.

bungeeist—the jumper, or the site manager/owner.

bungee jumping—the sport of jumping from a high platform while attached to an elastic bungee cord that prevents the jumper from hitting the ground.

bungee jumping system—the cords, carabiners, harnesses, webbing and ropes that are used as a unit in bungee jumping.

bungee kiss—a slight injury, usually a bruise or abrasion, to a jumper's face, neck, or limbs caused by coming in contact with the bungee cord.

cable—a strong, thick rope made of twisted wire used on a crane to raise and lower the jumping cage.

cage—the platform that hangs from the boom of a crane from which the bungee jumper leaps.

carabiner—the metal link that is used to connect various parts of the bungee jumping system. (See also oval, three-sided and D-shaped carabiner.)

catapulting—(see negative jump)

certified engineer—a person skilled in mathematical and scientific applications who is recognized by some agency as qualified to carry out certain responsibilities.

certified hot air balloon—a hot air balloon that has passed an inspection and has been certified as airworthy.

chest harness—a set of straps that are sewn together to fit around a jumper's chest, back, and arms. The harness is held in place by buckles and is used to attach a bungee jumper to bungee cords. The harness is used in conjunction with a seat harness.

choker—a steel cable used on a crane.

clip—(see carabiner)

commercial membership—one of two types of membership to the North American Bungee Association that includes benefits such as voting rights and participation in the insurance program. The fee for becoming a commercial member is $250.00 a year.

commercial pilot license—the license that is issued to a pilot when he is deemed to be qualified to operate an aircraft on a commercial basis. A pilot is required to obtain a private license before he can attempt to obtain a commercial license.

commercial site—a bungee jumping business that offers jumps to paying customers.

completed operations aggregate—the cumulative total that an insurance carrier will pay out on one policy from claims pertaining to loss, injury or damage that occurs after the jump as a result of the jump or any other product of the bungee site.

comprehensive general liability—the susceptibility to financial loss due to injury, damage, or loss to others. The term "comprehensive general" indicates inclusion of any possible liability.

continuous operation—operating for at least two days in a week for more than thirty-six weeks in a twelve month period.

continuous runner or loop—a continuous piece of material with no seams, a piece of material that has not been constructed from two or more pieces.

conventional crane—a mobile crane with a boom that is built with forty foot sections of solid lattice, and then the jib is built onto the boom. The conventional crane moves in a manner similar to a human arm. The base is like a shoulder, the boom is like the upper arm, and the jib is like the lower arm.

cord—the elastic rope that is used in bungee jumping that supports the weight of the jumper and prevents him from hitting the ground.

cord burns—(see bungee kiss)

cord system—(see bungee system)

cotton sheathing—the covering of a bungee cord that is made of cotton. Cotton sheathing is usually soft and dull vice the shiny and slick texture of the nylon sheathing.

count-down—the period of time preceding a jump in which the jump master or the spectators count down to zero and to the command "JUMP!"

covered cord—(see sheathed cord)

covert jump—a jump that regulating agencies are not suppose to know about because the execution of the jump is in non-compliance with some regulation(s).

crane—a machine with a long, swinging arm, for lifting and moving heavy weights.

crane operator—the person who controls the movement of the crane and its appendages.

crew—the people who are responsible for carrying out the operations of a bungee site.

cycle—an expression meaning a cord has been stretched and relaxed one time.

decertified hot air balloon—a balloon that has had the airworthiness certification voided, either voluntarily or involuntarily.

deductible—the part of an insurance claim that the claimant has to pay.

defined area—the area designated for the bungee jump by the owner or operator.

design specifications—the requirements of a piece of equipment in relation to its design.

diameter—the thickness of a cord or rope.

diaper seat harness—a seat harness that has a waist belt, then a second loop that pulls up from the back through the legs to form the leg loops.

distributor—the person who acts as a middle-man between the manufacturer and the consumer.

double-back buckles—a clasp used on harnesses on which the soft material is ran through the metal clasp one direction and then ran back the other direction to lessen the chances of the connection working loose.

double covered cord—(see double sheathed cord)

double sheathed cord—a bungee cord that has two layers of covering.

drift—loss of tension.

D-shaped carabiner—a carabiner that is shaped like a capitol "D". Its shape makes it a strong link because it carries the most stress on its long side. The long side is the strongest side because it is the side without the gate.

dual jump—(see tandem jump)

dynamic cord—a cylindrical rope that is designed to have some stretch, thirty five to forty five percent at failure.

dynamic load—the load placed on the rigging and attachments by the initial free fall of the jumper and the bouncing movements of the jumper.

elasticity—a measurement of the ability of a cord or rope to stretch.

elongation—the lengthening of the bungee cord.

engineering letter of approval—a document issued by the FAA that indicates the FAA's approval of modifications made to a hot air balloon, or any other aircraft. The letter is issued when the modifications are moderate.

envelope—the colorful bag that holds the hot air in a balloon.

envelope cables—the cords that attach the gondola to the envelope on a hot air balloon.

equator—an imaginary circle around the hot air balloon's envelope at its largest circumference on a horizontal plane.

expansion—(see elongation)

expense—a financial expenditure that is necessary to operate a business.

extended length—the length of the cord when it is extended the most that it will be during the current cycle.

eye—the loop that is placed on the end of a bungee cord to which the next link of the bungee system is attached.

FAA—(Federal Aviation Administration) the government agency responsible for controlling civilian and military air traffic and regulate air lines.

failure—the point at which a piece of equipment is unable to handle the increasing stress to which it is being subjected.

fall—the position of a jumper when he is between the platform and the end of the cord.

FAR—(Federal Aviation Regulations) the regulations set up by the FAA pertaining to air traffic and air lines.

Federal Aviation Administration—(see FAA)

Federal Aviation Regulations—(see FAR)

field approval—the formal recognition by the FAA of an aircraft's ability to safely fly.

field inspection—the inspection performed to determine if a field approval can be awarded.

field inspector—the person who performs the field inspection.

finished end—the end of a bungee cord that has been prepared to attach to the next link of the bungee jumping system.

flex cycle—(see cycle)

Flight Standards Division Manager—(see FSDO)

Flight Standards inspectors—(see field inspector)

Form 337—a document issued by the FAA that indicates the FAA's approval of modifications made to a hot air balloon, or any other aircraft. The form is issued when the modifications are minor.

franchise—the privilege of operating a commercial bungee site under the name of an already existing corporation. Normally, a percentage of the site's revenue is committed to the parent corporation.

free fall—the portion of a bungee jump that the jumper's movement is not yet influenced by the bungee cord.

free-flying balloon—a balloon that is not tethered and is free to fly with wind currents.

FSDO—(Flight Standards Division Manager) an agent of the FAA who manages a regional division of the FAA's Flight Standards.

full-body harness—a set of straps that are sewn together to fit around a jumper's back, stomach, shoulders, waist and crotch. The harness is held in place by buckles and is used to attach a bungee jumper to bungee cords. The harness can be one unit or can be two units, a seat harness and a chest harness, that are used as one unit.

gate—the part of a carabiner that opens to allow the carabiner to be attached to another piece of equipment.

gate junction—the part of a carabiner where the end of the gate touches the unmovable part of the carabiner.

general aggregate—the cumulative total that an insurance carrier will pay out on one policy from claims pertaining to loss, injury or damage that occurs at the time of the jump.

gondola—the structure beneath a hot air balloon for carrying passengers.

ground chief—the member of a bungee site's crew who oversees the efforts of the ground crew. The ground chief usually is under the direction of the jump master.

ground crew—the crew members whose efforts are concentrated on the ground efforts such as putting on and removing harnesses, weighing the jumpers, selling tickets, etc.

guidelines—recommendations or rules used as an industry standard.

half-way point—the point of the jump after the free fall but before the cord begins to expand.

hardware—any piece of equipment, or only the equipment that is made of very hard material such as metal.

harness—(see ankle harness, chest harness, full-body harness, or seat harness)

harness assembly—all of the equipment in the bungee system that is between the bottom end of the bungee cord and the jumper.

headache ball—the heavy ball that hangs on the cables from the boom of a crane.

head dunk—(see water dunk)

hernia—a condition of the bungee cord when the rubber pushes through the covering due to damage to the cord.

horizontal plane—parallel to the horizon.

hot air balloon—an aircraft that is driven by heated air and that looks like a giant balloon carrying a basket on its underside.

hot air balloon pilot—(see pilot)

hydraulic crane—a mobile crane with a boom that is telescopic. The boom is extended and retracted during use.

IABE—(see International Association of Bungee Enthusiasts)

individual certificate of insurance—a document provided to a bungee business that recognizes that the business is covered under a master insurance policy.

initial fall—the first fall of a bungee jump, usually the longest fall of the jump.

initial rebound—the first rebound of a bungee jump, usually the greatest rebound of the jump.

International Association of Bungee Enthusiasts—the initial name of the North American Bungee Association.

ISO simplification—the interpretation of which claims an insurance underwriter should reasonably be expected to cover as determined by the International Standards Organization.

jib—the secondary portion of the movable arm on a conventional crane.

jolt—jar or jerk felt by the balloon or jumper.

jump area—the maximum designed area in all directions for the movement of the jumper.

jumper—the person that jumps from a height with one end of a bungee cord attached to his body and the other end to the platform.

jumping cage—(see cage)

jumping shelf—(see shelf)

jumping system—(see bungee jumping system)

jump ledge—(see shelf)

jump master—the person who rides on the platform with, and coaches, the jumper; also may be the person who oversees the entire bungee operation.

jump point—the spot from which the jumper leaves the platform.

jump operator—(see operator, jump)

jump style—the manner in which the jumper leaves the platform. The style may be a front dive, back dive, feet-first jump, flip, etc.

jump zone—the area on the ground that is directly below the platform and the airspace that the jumper may occupy during a jump.

knotted rope—a rope that has knots tied in it approximately every foot that is used by the jumper to upright himself towards the end of a jump with ankles harnesses. The rope is attached on one end to the jumper's waist harness and the other end at the end of the bungee cord.

landing area—the surface area of the ground, pad, air bag or water directly under the platform onto which the jumper is lowered after the jump.

landing pad—the ground, pad, or air bag directly under the jump space.

lateral direction—the area measured at ninety degrees to the designed jump direction.

launch platform—(see platform)

"legal" site—a commercial bungee site that is in compliance with all pertinent regulations and rules.

leg loops—the part of a seat harness that wrap around the legs.

lessee—the person or business that leases property from the person who owns the property.

liability—susceptibility to financial loss due to injury, loss or damage to others.

liability insurance—insurance taken out against injury, loss or damage to others.

life cycle—the number of times that a cord can be stretched and relaxed before it should be retired.

life lines—cords or cables used as a safety feature to catch a jump master or jumper should he fall from a height unintentionally.

link—a carabiner or screw link; or any component of the bungee system that connects any other two or more components.

litigation—legal action.

load—the stress to which any equipment is subjected.

loaded length—the length of the bungee cord when extended to its fullest designed length.

local certification office—an office of the Flights Standards Division of the FAA that interfaces with the local owners of aircrafts.

locking carabiner—a carabiner that has a nut that tightens over the gate junction to lock the gate shut.

locking design—a feature on a carabiner that acts as a back-up to the primary closure mechanism.

long axis—lengthwise.

loop—(cord end)

loop, continuous—(see continuous runner)

lowering system—(see retrieval system)

manufacturer—the person or company who produces a product.

margin of error—(see safety margin)

master—(see jump master)

master insurance policy—a blanket insurance policy provided for an organization and that is available to individual subscribers who are members of the organization.

mentor—a person who provides guidance to another.

military specification—standards set by the military for products manufactured for the military's use.

MIL-SPEC—(see military specification)

mobile crane—a crane that has wheels on its base and can be prepared for transportation to a different location with relative ease.

modification—a partial alteration or change.

moored aircraft—any lighter-than-air object that is operated under FAA FAR 101. A moored aircraft may refer to a hot air balloon that has been decertified for the purpose of bungee jumping without being subject to the regulations associated with operating a certified hot air balloon.

mooring lines—(see tether lines)

multi-cord system—a bungee jumping system that involves more than one cord at one time.

NABA—(see North American Bungee Association)

negative jump—a type of bungee jump where a group of people hold down a jumper on the ground while the platform, to which the jumper is attached via a bungee cord, is raised. This results in a taut bungee cord. The group of people release the jumper and he is hurdled towards the platform.

New Zealand/Australian Standards—the industry standards that are used mainly in Europe.

non-locking carabiner—a carabiner that does not have a feature to lock the swing gate shut.

North American Bungee Association—the association that is currently led by Thomas Woodard.

nut—the part of a carabiner that screws over the gate junction.

nylon sheathing—the covering of a bungee cord that is made of nylon. Nylon sheathing is usually shiny and slick vice the soft and dull texture of the cotton sheathing.

Occupational Safety and Health Administration—(see OSHA)

offset jib—a jib that is capable of movement.

one piece wrap-around seat harness—a seat harness that uses a continuous loop of webbing for the leg loops and the waist belt.

operating manual—the document containing the procedures and forms for the operation of all bungee jumping activities and equipment.

operational approval—(see field approval)

operator, site—the manager of a bungee site.

operator, jump—a person who assists the jump master to prepare a jumper for jumping, or who operates the system that lowers/raise the jumper.

OSHA—(Occupational Safety and Health Administration) the agency responsible for insuring that all employees have a safe and healthy environment in which to work.

oval carabiner—a carabiner that is shaped in an oval.

panic handle—the lengths of webbing that run between the jumper and the bungee cord. The jumper can hang on to these straps if he becomes frightened and needs something to hang on to because they do not stretch and won't cause burns to to rapid expansion.

parabola—the locus of points equidistant from a fixed line and a fixed point not on the line.

participant—commercial jumper.

path—the line along which a jumper moves during a jump.

percent of elongation—the percent of the relaxed length of a cord that is equal to the delta of the cord's current length and its relaxed length.

performance specifications—the requires for a piece of equipment in relation to its performance.

permanent crane—a crane that requires a foundation and extensive construction effort to erect and is relatively difficult to transport to another location.

permanent platform—the area attached to a high structure from which jumper falls or jumps.

permits—a formal written order giving permission to a business to operate in a specific arena.

personal protective equipment—equipment that protects the site employees and jumpers, such as gloves, helmets, life lines, etc.

pilot—the person who is flying the hot air balloon.

platform—the equipment from which a bungee jump is executed such as a crane, hot air balloon, bridge or tower; also may refer to the jumping shelf.

platform assembly—the jumping shelf and its related hardware.

platform height—the distance between the ground and the point from which the jumper leaps.

premium—the payment to an insurance company from a person or business for insurance coverage.

preparation area—(see staging area)

products aggregate—the cumulative total that an insurance carrier will pay out on one policy from claims pertaining to loss, injury or damage that occurs from use of products other than the bungee jump such as tee-shirts, concessions, and videos.

prusik loop/knot—a special knot that allows one cord to attach to a straight cord. The knot is self-tightening and allows the first cord to easily move on the length of the second cord without untying the knot.

public area—(see spectator area)

pulley—a wheel with a grooved rim in which a rope can run, and so change the direction of the pull.

pulley system—the set of equipment, usually including a pulley and rope, used to raise or lower the jumper after the jumper has stopped bouncing.

ratio—relation in degree or number between two similar things.

raw ends—ends of a bungee cord that have not been finished in any way.

rebound—the portions of the bungee jump in which the jumper is moving in an upward direction.

rebound capability—the ability of a bungee cord to send a jumper upwards after a fall during a jump.

recovery—(see retrieval)

recovery area—an area next to the jump zone, where the jumper may recover from the jump before returning to the spectator area.

recovery vessel—the water vessel, such as a boat, onto which the jumper is lowered after jumping over water. The recovery vessel should have a landing pad.

redundant system—a bungee system that for every component/link there is a back-up component/link.

relaxed length—the length of a bungee cord when it is subject to zero stress.

retire—discard or quit using.

retrieval—to lower or raise a jumper to a solid surface after he has stopped bouncing.

retrieval system—the hardware that is used to lower or raise a jumper to a solid surface after he has stopped bouncing.

revenue—money that a commercial site receives in turn for providing the resources for a bungee jump or for providing other concessions.

rigging—the hardware used in the bungee system and its attachment to the platform.

rigging system—(see bungee system)

runner, continuous—(see continuous runner)

safety belt—a belt designed to fit around the waist of a person which can be attached to either an anchor point or safety line.

safety equipment—any equipment that is used to protect a jumper, spectator or crew member from a potential danger.

safety factor—a feature that is intended to increase the safety of the jumpers, crew members, or spectators. This may include safety gear, a safety space, or a safety ratio.

safety gear—any equipment that is used to aid in the protection of the jumpers, crew members, or spectators.

safety harness—an assembly to be worn by an jump operator. It is designed to be attached to a safety line and prevent the jump operator from falling from the platform.

safety hook—a hook with a latch to prevent equipment or load from accidentally slipping off the hook.

safety line—a line used to connect a safety harness or belt to an anchor point.

safety margin—(see safety space)

safety ratio—a number derived by dividing the breaking strength of a piece of equipment by the load to which the piece of equipment is being subjected. If a bungee cord has a breaking strength of five hundred pounds and it is being subjected to a load of fifty pounds, the safety factor is ten.

safety space—a space extending beyond the jump zone as a safety factor.

safe working load—(see SWL)

sand-bagging—a special jump in which one jumper wears the harnesses in a normal fashion, and then bear hugs either a sandbag or a second person who is not fastened to the cords in any way. The duo jumps from a platform, and when the cord has reached full extension, the sandbag or second person is dropped to the landing area. This causes the jumper to rebound to a point higher than the platform. This type of jump is not recommended because the path of the jumper is very difficult to predict, and the jumper can easily hit the platform or other hard objects. Also, the sandbag or second person can be torn from the grasp of the jumper prematurely due to the tremendous velocity created by the sandbag or person's inertia. The sandbag or person may land in an undesirable location and injure people on the ground as well as possibly the person who has been dropped.

scoop—a cloth that shields a side of the opening of the hot air balloon envelope near to where the flame is located. The scoop hangs downward from the opening, and is commonly used when the balloon is tethered to assist in controlling the balloon's movements.

screw gate type carabiner—(see screw link)

screw link—a carabiner that is closed by screwing a nut over the opening (gate) of the carabiner. Another common type of carabiner has a spring-loaded swinging gate that is locked shut by a nut screwed over the end of the gate.

seat harness—a set of straps that are sewn together to fit around a jumper's waist, back and crotch. The harness is held in place by buckles and is used to attach a bungee jumper to bungee cords. The harness is used in conjunction with a chest harness.

shackle—(see carabiner)

sheathed cord—a bungee cord with the rubber interior covered with one or two layers of either cotton or nylon braid.

shelf—the small ledge on which the jumper stands immediately before jumping. The shelf is different than a platform in that a shelf is just large enough to stand on, such as the diving board attached to a bridge railing or the piece of wood attached to the side of the balloon basket, and the platform is the structure to which the shelf is attached, such as the crane, hot air balloon or bridge. However, the two terms may be used interchangeably.

shoulder strap—(see chest harness)

side-to-side clearance—the clear air space required to allow for the swinging and bouncing movements of the jumper during the jump.

single cord system—a bungee jumping system that uses only one bungee cord at any one time.

single covered cord—(see single sheathed cord)

single sheathed cord—a bungee cord that is covered by only one layer of covering.

site—the location of a bungee jumping operation. Site may refer to the piece of land or to the business entity.

site owner—the person(s) who own the bungee business. In some cases, it may refer to the person who owns the land on which the site is operated.

sit harness—(see seat harness)

skill level—the amount of ability required to perform a bungee jump, or the amount of bungee jumping ability that a jumper possess.

sling—any component of the bungee system that bears a load and that is constructed from webbing or similar material. Usually a sling is used to attach the bungee system to the platform.

soda can grab—a special jump in which a jumper attempts to come close enough to the ground to pick a soda pop can from the ground or from the hand of a person standing on the ground.

software—equipment that is made of material that is soft or flexible.

special jumps—(see stunts)

staging area—a commercial bungee site can be divided into three

areas: the jump zone, the staging area, and the spectator area. The staging area is where the pre-jump and post-jump activities, such as the fitting of the harnesses, are performed.

standardized approved exclusions—the types of insurance claims that an insurance underwriter is not required to cover because those claims are considered to be non-standard. The International Standards Organization is the agency that determines the standardized approved exclusions.

standards—(see guidelines)

static cord—a cylindrical rope with very low stretch, only fifteen to twenty percent at failure.

static extended length—the length of the bungee cord when the jumper is hanging from the cord but is no longer moving up and down.

static line—(see static cord)

static weight, jumper's—the weight of the jumper when he is not moving. Static weight is used when referring to the stress produced by the jumper when he is still vice the stress produced when his weight is multiplied by his velocity during a jump.

STC—(Supplemental Type Certificate) a document issued by the FAA that indicates the FAA's approval of modifications made to a hot air balloon, or any other aircraft. The STC is issued when the modifications are major.

stitching—sewing that is used to attach two or more loose end of software.

stop—the point at the bottom of a fall during a jump.

stress—an applied force.

stunt—any jump that removes one or more common safety factor.

Supplemental Type Certificate—(see STC)

swami belt—a type of seat harness that is not as complex as the seat harness commonly used for a jump.

swan dive—a style of bungee jumping in which the jumper faces away from the jumping platform and then falls forward and headfirst with the arms spread out to the side.

SWL—Safe Working Load, the maximum rated load as determined by the manufacture which can be safely handled under specified conditions, by a machine, equipment or component of the bungee system.

tandem jump—a special jump in which two jumpers are attached to the bungee cord and to each other, then jump as if they were one jumper.

temporary site—a bungee site that is designed to set up and tear down easily, and to transport to a new location with relative ease. A hot air balloon is often used in a temporary site.

tensile strength—(see breaking strength)

testing authority—an organization qualified and authorized to test the performance of bungee equipment.

tethered balloon—a balloon that is tied to the ground vice allowed to free fly.

tether anchors—the heavy objects, such as vehicles or buildings, to which the tether ropes are tied when a balloon is tethered.

tether lines—(see tether ropes)

tether ropes—the lines used to tie a hot air balloon to the ground when the balloon is tethered.

three-sided carabiner—

tower—a type of bungee platform. If a platform is not a hot air balloon, crane, or bridge, then it is usually categorized as a tower.

tower crane—a permanent crane that is used for the construction of very tall buildings. The tower crane looks like a giant "T". It is normally not used for bungee jumping because it is not mobile and it is very expenses to lease or buy.

training—the instruction that a customer receives prior to jumping, or the instruction that a crew member or site operator receives prior to working at the site.

type certified product—an aircraft that an agent of the FAA has inspected and certified as airworthy.

Type I MIL-SPEC cord—the type of MIL-SPEC cord that is referred to in this book.

UIAA—(Union International Alpinism Association) the association responsible for setting standards for mountain climbing and rescue equipment.

ultimate elongation—the elongation at failure.

uncovered cord—(see unsheathed cord)

Union International Alpinism Association—(see UIAA)

unloaded length—(see relaxed length)

unsheathed cord—a bungee cord that is not covered and the rubber interior is exposed.

unstretched length—(see relaxed length)

velcro—an attachment that uses two types of material that catches onto each other and holds.

vertical plane—perpendicular to the horizon.

waist belt—the part of the seat harness that wraps around the jumper's waist.

waiver—a form that is signed by commercial jumpers that releases the bungee site from liability due to injury, loss or damage to the jumper due to the bungee jump, and that forces the jumper to recognize the potential danger involved with bungee jumping.

water dunk—a special jump in which the jumper's head enters a body of water when the cord is fully extended.

webbing—a very strong strap that is sometimes used to attach the bungee cords to the platform, or to attach the harnesses to the cords. Webbing is usually flat and is usually made from nylon.

whip—to change directions quickly.

whipping—very strong string that is wrapped tightly around a cord to hold other software to the cord.

workman's compensation—an insurance purchased to cover employees in case of work related injuries, loss or damage.

wrap-around seat harness—(see one piece wrap-around seat harness)

"W" stitch—a type of stitching that looks like two "W""s, one upside down to the other, with a box around them.

zone—(see jump zone)

zoning regulations—the building restrictions in an area of a city or town.

Bibliography

Accardi, Thomas C., "'Bungee Jumping' from Balloons" memo, Director of Flight Standards Service, AFS-1, Federal Aviation Administration, Washington, DC, May 30, 1991.

American Bungee Association informational cover sheet, Huntington Beach, California, August, 1991.

Armstrong, Rick, interviews, President of Boing Bungee, Inc., Escondido, California, June 1991—October 1991.

Bell, Charlie, interviews, Air Boulder, Boulder, Colorado, March 1991—November 1991.

A.J. Hackett Bungy, interview, Cairns, Queensland, Australia, March 1991.

Brown, Greg, interview, Bungy Zone, Nanaimo, British Columbia, Canada, March 1991.

Bungee Cords, newsletter for the North American Bungee Association, vol. 1, no. 1-9 (all articles), January 1991—October 1991.

Bungee Jumping, 300-8-1, Revision 1, Georgia Statute, Atlanta, Georgia, October 21, 1991.

"'Bungee Jumping' From Hot Air Balloons" FAA memo, *Skylines*, newsletter for the Balloon Federation of America, vol. 18, no. 12, p. 1, December 1990.

Bungee Jumping Systems informational packet, Adrenalin Adventures, Boulder, Colorado, March 1991.

"Bungee jumping to take off in Idaho Spring canyon," Fort Collins Coloradoan, Fort Collins, Colorado, February 26, 1991.

"Business Bulletin, Bungee Laws Bounce Up," *The Wall Street Journal*, Eastern Edition, White Oak, Maryland, September 19, 1991, p. A-1.

Cassady, John H., "Manned Moored Balloons—FAR Parts 91 & 101" memo, Assistant Chief Counsel of Regulations & Enforcement Division, AGC-200, of the Federal Aviation Administration, June 28, 1984.

Danelski, David, and Darrell Santschi, "Bungee jumper from balloon falls to death," The Press-Enterprise, Riverside, California, October 28, 1991, p. A-8.

Davis, Rick, "Eagle Sports Writer Takes Ultimate Plunge," Butler Eagle, Butler, Pennsylvania, Sports section, August 27, 1991, p. 13, 14.

Deggans, Eric, "Bungee jumpers take the plunge into daring quest for ultimate rush'," The Pittsburgh Press, Pittsburgh, Pennsylvania, September 18, 1991, p. N-1, N-6.

Diamond, Michael R., and Julie L. Williams, *How to Incorporate: A Handbook for Entrepreneurs and Professionals*, New York, John Wiley & Sons, 1987.

Federal Aviation Regulations (FAR), Seattle, Washington, Aviation Supplies & Academics, Inc. (ASA), 1990.

Finocchiaro, Carl, computerized trajectory analysis, President of Bungee Jumping Colorado, Inc., Denver, Colorado, January 1991.

—"Bungee Jumping Colorado! Bungee Jumping Technical Information," February 1991.

Gottschalk, Kurt, interview, Balloon Federation of America, Pittsburgh, Pennsylvania, August 1990.

Greenwald, Jim, interview, Oklahoma Department of Labor, Oklahoma City, Oklahoma, October 1991.

Habuda, Janice L., "Bungee jumper to bounce back: Injured daredevil undaunted," The Buffalo News, Buffalo, New York, August 2, 1991.

Hamilton, Tom, "Bungee Jumping: Look Carefully Before Leaping for Quick Riches," *Balloon Life*, vol. 6, no. 5, May 1991, p. 12-15.

—"Preflight, Bungee Update," *Balloon Life*, vol. 6, no. 7, July 1991, p. 8.

Hardie, Jeff, "How to have your life flash by in three second and 145 feet," Washington Times, Washington, DC, Sports section, 1991, p. D-1, D-2.

Hase', Doug, interview, President of Adrenaline Adventures, Boulder, Colorado, October 1990.

Hatch, Joseph P., proposal of insurance to the North American Bungee Association, Joseph P. Hatch, Inc. for Frontier Insurance Company, Monticello, New York, August 23, 1991.

Hogan, Denise, "Bungee Jumping on the Rogue River," *Oregon Coast*, vol. 10, no. 4, July/August 1991, p. 99-101.

Howe, Jennifer, "Elastic enjoyment: Bungee jumping in KC," The Kansas City Star, Kansas City, Kansas, Style section, September 13, 1991, p. E-1, E-6.

"Hulsey v. Elsinore Parachute Center" summary, Superior Court, Riverside County, California, May 16, 1985.

Huspeni, Dennis, "EEEEAAAAHHH!!!!! Reporter takes bungee plunge," Fort Collins Coloradoan, Fort Collins, Colorado, Choice section, August 18, 1991, p. C-1, C-2.

Kalakuka, Christine, copy of an Express Assumption of Risk Agreement and Medical Statement, Balloon Excelsior, Inc., Oakland, California, July 1991.

Kockelman, John, and Peter Kockelman, interviews, video and informational packet, owners of Bungee Adventures, Mountain View, California, March 1991—July 1991.

Laslavic, Thomas E., "Bungee Jumpers Take Leap toward Safety," Cranberry Eagle, Pennsylvania, July 24, 1991, p. 2.

Lawton, Pat, interviews, Bungee Express, Valencia, Pennsylvania, February 1991—July 1991.

Mailer, Larry, interviews, Manager of Product Support Group Domestic of the Small Airplane Directorate of the Federal Aviation Administration, Kansas City, Missouri, March 1991.

Masullo, Gina, "Bungee business ready to take big leap," The Times Herald Record, New York, The Region section, May 28, 1991, p. 4.

McCullen, Kevin, "Bungee-jumping regulations coming," Rocky Mountain News, Denver, Colorado, September 22, 1991, p. 7, 16.

Meyers, Jeff of Los Angeles Times, "BUNGEEEEEEEEE, Gee-whiz sport bounces jumper out of a balloon," Fort Collins Coloradoan, Fort Collins, Colorado, Choice section, June 6, 1991, p. B-1, B-2.

—"FAA Gives Boost to Bungee Jumpers," Los Angeles Times, Los Angeles, California, June 27, 1991,

"Military Specification MIL-C-5651D: Cord, Elastic, Exerciser and Shock Absorber, for Aeronautical Use," Systems Engineering and Standardization Department of the Naval Air Engineering Center, Lakehurst, New Jersey, March 2, 1977.

Mills, Jorden, interviews, President of Big Bounce Bungee, Inc., Kingston, New York, July 1991—August 1991.

Morrison, Dan, "Rubberband Man," American Way, p. 18-21, August, 1991.

Nel, Ricco, "News Release Concerning the Bungee Accident in Norway," President of the American Bungee Association, Huntington Beach, California, August 29, 1991.

—Interviews, August 1990—August 1991.

Parish, Larry, interviews, President of Vertigo Ventures, Kansas City, Kansas, June 1991—November 1991.

Raleigh, Duane, "Tie Into Something Comfortable: Harnesses for All Types of Climbing," Climbing, no. 129, December 1991/January 1992, p. 89-97.

Schindler, Charlie, and Eric Gruber, interviews and more, owners of Bungee Ho!, Phoenix, Arizona, September 1991—December 1991.

Scott, Al, "Hearing on Bungee Jumping Regulations Moved" memo, Commissioner of Georgia Department of Labor, Atlanta, Georgia, October 23, 1991.

"South Africa, Bungee jumper killed," The Press-Enterprise, Riverside, California, October 27, 1991, p. A-2.

Stone, Dan, interviews, President of Balloons Over Charlotte, Charlotte, North Carolina, August 1990—October 1991.

Tanner, Morgan, "Attack of the Beach Blanket Death Divers from Hell: The Real Story," Soldier of Fortune, March 1991, p. 41-43.

Tessada, Carolyn, completed Federal Aviation Administration Form 337 and interviews, President of Mystical Balloon Flights, Las Vegas, Nevada, February 1991—July 1991.

Thigpen, David E., "Bungee Jumping Comes of Age," *Time*, April 15, 1991, p. 50-51.

—"The Ultimate Leap of Faith," *Time*, April 23, 1990, p. 75.

Total Rebound informational packet, Total Rebound, San Francisco, California, 1991.

Vertige Aventures catalog and interview, Vertige Aventures, Grenoble, France, 1989.

Vetter, Craig, "The Fabulous, Bouncing Kockelman Brothers," *Outside*, vol. 16, no. 7, July 1991, p. 47-51, 104-107.

—"Rubber Jump," *Playboy*, September 1990, p. 98-100, 160-162.

Weinel, John E., Rock-N-Rescue catalog, J.E. Weinel, Inc., Valencia, Pennsylvania, 1990.

—Interviews, February 1991—October 1991.

Wilkenson, John, interview, President of Total Rebound, San Francisco, California, September 1991.

Wilson, Calvin, "Man, 81, takes plunge — possibly into bungee history", The Kansas City Star, Kansas City, Kansas, Johnson Country/Metro section, October 7, 1991.

Withycombe, William, for Thomas C. Accardi, "'Bungee Jumping' From Hot Air Balloons" memo, Acting Director of Flight Standards Service, AFS-1, US Department of Transportation, Federal Aviation Administration, Washington, DC, October 3, 1990.

Woodard, Thomas J., "Bungee Jumping related death today in Perris, California" press release, President of North American Bungee Association, Park City, Utah, October 27, 1991.

—Interviews, June 1991—November 1991.

Zemitis, Martin, interviews, President of Bungee Jumping System, Inc., Berkley, California, March 1991—August 1991.

Zlateff, Daniel, interview, President of Z-Boing, Orchard Park, NY, September 1991.

About the Author

On a rainy weekend in August of 1990, Nancy Frase packed her toothbrush and tent on the back of her Honda Nighthawk motorcycle and drove the 425 miles from Washington, DC to Charlotte, North Carolina. Her soul purpose was to bungee jump from a hot air balloon. She had never seen commercial bungee cords and had never been close to a hot air balloon. Two minutes after her first jump, she decided that this crazy sport would inevitably become a part of her life.

She immediately began researching the sport in an effort to start her own commercial bungee site from a hot air balloon. In October, the FAA published a memo that made opening such a site very difficult. She centered her efforts on working with the FAA to resolve the conflict.

A Colorado-based FAA official suggested organizing and focusing the energies of the industry's members in response to that suggestion, Nancy founded the bungee newsletter titled "Bungee Cords." The first issue of "Bungee Cords" was mailed out Christmas, 1990. The newsletter provided communication within the bungee industry, and was the means of advertisement for a significant meeting.

The last weekend of March, a group of ten bungee enthusiasts met in Pittsburgh, Pennsylvania. One outcome of the meeting was the formation of the North American Bungee Association of Bungee Enthusiasts, now known as the North American Bungee Association. Nancy was appointed founding president. She was active in the association through October 1991, when she turned over her responsibilities to other association members.

Nancy grew up in Colorado and Nebraska, and graduated from a Christian college in Oklahoma. She is currently living in Herndon, Virginia with a household of interesting characters, including Samantha the boa constrictor, Megan the kitten, and Morti the iguana. She is preparing for a career as a police officer.